insure the BAG

Not all bags are created equal

Ashley Mckoy

insure the BAG

Not all bags are created equal

Insure The Bag
© 2024 by Ashley McKoy

ISBN-13: 979-8-218-45374-9 Paperback
979-8-218-45375-6 Hardcover
Library Of Congress Control Number: 2024913913

Printed in the United States of America.

ITB Publishing House
Jersey City, New Jersey

Dedication & Acknowledgements

To my grandmother Selestine, who has since passed but whose spirit will always live inside of me; killing them with kindness is something that you taught me and I'll never forget it for as long as I shall live!

To my mother Sandy, you have immensely showered me with soft and tough love; each equipping me for the life that was ahead of me. I may not have always understood every move you made as a mother but it's all coming together. Obviously, "be the best that you can be, even if you're a bum, be the best bum," is embedded in my head, lol. So, the best me is what they shall see!

To my father Stephon, thank you for instilling from a very early age that being "The Real McKoy" is not on me, it's in me! That there is nothing that I can't accomplish and do! To you I'm the best thing since sliced bread, and I'll always love you so much for that!

Preface

This memoir chronicles the journey of overcoming obstacles, facing challenges and demonstrating unwavering perseverance.

Not all areas of your life hold the same significance, just like not all bags are created equal. Each aspect you wish to invest in has its own unique qualities. Understanding that we tend to resonate with advice that aligns with our current mindset, feel free to start with the chapter that resonates with you the most. As priorities shift with time and age, this book Isn't meant to be read in a specific order. You can explore the subjects that call to you, based on the season of life you're in today.

This book doesn't aim to impose its advice on you, but rather to establish a connection and understanding by sharing my personal experiences. It's a book that says, 'you're not alone, we're in this together.

This book consists of 9 chapters, as the number 9 holds significant meaning. It symbolizes completion, but not as a definitive end; rather, it signifies the fulfillment of one cycle, paving the way for the initiation of the next. It serves as a reminder of life's continuous ebb and flow.

Table of Contents

"Not everything that holds value is tangible, however, everything has its inherent worth."

Tangibility is the perception of touch, but the ability to believe in the things we've yet to grasp?

That's strengthening your mental capacity!

("Alexa, play Beyonce- Alien Superstar")

Believing in tangible things comes naturally to us because we can see, touch and feel them. Many people find comfort in this belief since it seems like the safest option. They say that if something is visible, they can aspire to become it or achieve it. But what about the intangible things? What about the dreams we obsessively and imaginatively envision—the ones that seem wild? I've always been taught that if you never ask, the answer is always no. Similarly, aiming for the sky might get you to the top of a building but shooting for the stars allows you to surpass the entire sky. All of this is heavily influenced by our mindset. Strengthening our mental capacity is crucial as it sharpens our ideas, enhances our agility and broadens our thinking. Many have told me that I possess a vivid imagination which would make me a perfect fit for the Disney Animation department—a job I believe would've been truly amazing, might I add.

Considering all of that, I see it as a compliment. I've always preferred to be recognized as the sharpest tool in the box, a strategic planner, a technical and analytical thinker and so on, rather than anything else.

My father instilled in me the importance of having both brains and brawn, emphasizing the value of strength combined with wit. Even at the age of 4, while I could have been reading nursery rhymes like "Twinkle, Twinkle, Little Star," I was engrossed in reading the New York Times word for word. These early experiences truly shaped my mind. I learned from a young age that the more knowledge you possess across various subjects, the better equipped you are to navigate the world and interact with remarkable individuals.

You've probably heard the saying "the mind is a terrible thing to waste," and it holds true. Once your brain and mental state deteriorate, many other crucial aspects follow suit. That is why it's important not only to focus on tangible things we can see and feel but also to place importance on our thought processes, the perspectives of others and how they collectively influence our journey through life.

Throughout my career, I've had the privilege of meeting and engaging with a vast number of individuals and it has allowed me to personally witness the significance and value they attribute to tangible possessions they have worked hard to acquire and accomplish. These include homes, businesses, as well as cherished pets and even the consideration of life insurance among many other aspects.

This particular interest serves as one of the primary motivations behind my decision to write and share this content with you. Specifically, my reason for penning this book stems from my extensive experience in servicing clients' insurance needs on a daily basis spanning from significant to minor concerns. This has granted me valuable insights into how people navigate their daily lives. It's intriguing to observe that individuals willingly invest in and insure their lives for the future, prepare their cars for accidents or damages and safeguard their homes against various risks such as fire, theft and natural disasters. However, they often overlook investing in and ensuring their current day-to-day existence which is essential for leading a better, healthier and more fulfilling life.

Generally, people seek insurance to provide peace of mind for themselves and their loved ones in the face of unforeseen events. However, they often neglect to invest in their own quality of life. In the realm of business, insurance plays a significant role in perpetuating the wealth gap with the rich leveraging their advantages while the poor struggle to access such resources. Surprisingly, life operates on a similar principle except the insurance policy is you—the individual. Just as investing in insurance can make a significant difference in business, investing in ourselves can profoundly impact our lives. Taking ownership of our lives and making the necessary changes and adjustments is crucial for witnessing meaningful transformation.

My ultimate aspiration in striving to create a purposeful and successful book is that you prioritize investing in yourself. Let this next season and however many more it may take, revolve around "you"—yes, you! It's time to navigate through life with yourself in mind. In the past, I fell into the habit of prioritizing others' needs while neglecting my own. However, with time, I realized that this approach was neither productive nor praiseworthy, despite what we may believe.

It's crucial to make yourself a priority in your own life and unapologetically acknowledge that neglecting self-care will inevitably impact your ability to serve others effectively. The first step you need to take is developing and embracing your intuition. Often, we seek advice from others regarding personal situations but deep down, our gut feeling is usually spot-on. Sometimes what we think we need, we already possess!

If we constantly shape our lives based solely on the opinions of others, we might never discover our true selves or have confidence in our own decisions. When you have a strong sense of self-doubts fade away. Maintain mental clarity in one aspect: you may never be enough for the wrong person, place or thing. However, you will always be more than enough for what is specifically meant for you—something carefully planned or conceived with a purpose.

Avoid losing yourself in the expectations of others but always be open to listening to what they have to say. Filter and retain the valuable insights while discarding the negative ones. Consider everything including the words shared within this book. I'm not urging you to accept them without question but rather to apply them to your life as you see fit.

While insuring your properties, homes, cars, pets and the people dear to you is undoubtedly important—something I assist individuals with every day. It holds even greater significance to place value on the intangible aspects of your life. Love, personal growth through trials, accountability, financial freedom, spirituality, family, friends, emotional and mental well-being and finding balance—these elements though not physically tangible, greatly influence the course of your life.

Amidst the multitude of voices clamoring with differing opinions and the ever-expanding realm of social media where everyone seems to claim expertise in almost everything, it's essential to remember that nobody knows you better than yourself. Embarking on a journey of self-awareness enables you to invest not only in your overall well-being but also in the areas that will enhance your quality of life, all at your own pace.

This is precisely why I emphasize that this book is not intended to be read in any particular order because priorities naturally shift over time and with age. I encourage you to begin by engaging with the chapters that resonate with you most at this stage of your life before exploring others, allowing the process to unfold organically. As mentioned earlier, our minds often gravitate towards what is tangible before we can truly grasp the uncharted paths. Our mindset reflects our current possessions and perceived needs, yet it holds the potential to unlock our truest yet-to-be-achieved abilities.

Let me share a quick example that illustrates how investing in life insurance relates to life in general, (I had to include some insurance tips, as expected!). Investing in life insurance for the future, particularly for when you pass away, is undeniably crucial as you might have heard from various sources. This type of policy involves investing a portion of your income while you're alive, serving as a financial resource for your family by providing a death benefit that replaces your income after you're gone. However, what some people may not be aware of is that life insurance also offers living benefits. To keep it concise, certain riders such as those for terminal and chronic illness, may allow you to access a portion of your death benefit to cover medical bills and nursing care, depending on specific health conditions and time frames.

In this book, each chapter symbolizes a bag that you can safeguard and insure. Remember, the essence of insurance is to protect your assets including yourself. Similar to a life insurance policy, these chapters represent your living benefits. So, make the most of these living benefits while you're alive by investing in the legacy you will leave behind, much like paying premiums toward your death benefit.

Success can be measured in various ways and it varies based on the specific aspects of life you seek to enhance. In this book, you will find valuable content that caters to a wide range of areas. Keeping this in mind, I will provide insights and advice on nine key areas that often don't receive as much intentional focus in our daily lives but should.

Having shared all of that, I encourage you to approach this book with an open mind taking the time to absorb the content and reflecting on each chapter. Remember to be patient and avoid rushing through the material. Allow yourself moments of deep thought as you delve into each bag within the book.

What you choose to do with the insights you gain is entirely up to you but it's essential to recognize that repeating the same actions will yield the same results, most similar to insanity. This is your moment, marking the beginning of a new season that will unleash the best version of yourself. Consistency is the key to transforming mediocrity into excellence but as we journey towards consistency, let's remain mindful of conforming only to those things that resonate with our truest selves. Get ready to embark on this transformative journey, and insure-the-bag!

The Accountability Bag

Accountability is a significant concept that can have a broad impact on various aspects of your life. However, I want to focus specifically on self-accountability, encompassing both your thoughts and your actions. I vividly recall the moment I discovered Jack Canfield's book, "The Success Principles - How To Get From Where You Are to Where You Want To Be." The first chapter delves deep into the concept of accountability and it profoundly affected me. I had never encountered such a direct and transformative exploration of this area before, and I can honestly say it completely changed my mindset.

I distinctly remember a particular part of the book where Jack Canfield mentioned complaining about traffic as a reason for being late to work. At that moment I felt personally called out (laughs) because I was living in Jersey City and commuting to my Grandfather's insurance agency in South Orange. I would often blame the terrible traffic for my lateness which was indeed a legitimate issue. However, after reading that section in the chapter, I realized that Jack was absolutely right. I needed to leave earlier allowing myself extra time to account for potential traffic delays and still arrive on time. From that point forward and even to this day I started evaluating every area of my life that required adjustments, seeking ways in which I could take personal control over the outcomes. This realization was a complete game changer for me. It ignited a newfound sense of purpose in my decision making, actions and more.

How often do we hold others accountable for our trials, mistakes, negative outcomes, failures and lack of happiness? Honestly, I have done it in the past. Even today, many entrepreneurs believe they must strictly follow someone else's views or steps in order to achieve success. Both men and women often place the burden of their happiness solely on someone else; in relationships for example, expecting that person to be responsible for their well-being. People frequently attribute their current unhappiness to their past yet fail to take the necessary steps toward creating a better future.

There are numerous examples I could share but the bottom line is that you bear full responsibility for yourself. A powerful quote by Martin Luther King Jr. states, "you can't prevent birds from flying over your head, but you can prevent them from building a nest in your hair." Life presents many uncontrollable factors yet how you respond, the actions you take, the thoughts you engage in and the emotions you choose to embrace are entirely within your control. You are the one accountable and no one else carries that responsibility. Let's now explore the importance of holding yourself accountable for your thoughts and actions.

Thoughts and actions are deeply interconnected, acting as a reflection of one another. Your actions tend to align with your prevailing thoughts; therefore, it is crucial to take accountability for the thoughts that dominate your mind. For instance, if you believe you are incapable of accomplishing something, you are less likely to make the effort to try. As a result, feelings of frustration, defeat and unworthiness arise, accompanied by the bitter sensation of witnessing someone else achieve what you believed you could have done.

Your mind has the power to influence your actions. If you genuinely believe in your ability to achieve something, it becomes highly probable that you will succeed. Ultimately even if you have exhausted all efforts and still fall short of your desired outcome, you can take satisfaction in knowing that you did not begin with a defeated mindset. It may simply be that the circumstances were not aligned in your favor at that particular moment.

The truth does not negate reality nor is it confined by it. It may be a fact that you have limited resources, belong to a minority group or face greater challenges and obstacles compared to others just to have an opportunity. However, these factors do not render your goals or dreams impossible to achieve. You must shatter the limitations that you have allowed to reside in your mind and heart, including those spoken into your life by family members, partners, society, religious institutions or even self-imposed limitations. If I had embraced the notion that the odds were stacked against me on my journey to becoming who I am today, you would not be holding this book in your hands.

You are not accountable for the words spoken about you or to you by others. However, you bear responsibility for how you respond—what you say, think and do about it. Taking ownership of all aspects of your life means removing the victim crown and donning the crown of a participant. You are not a victim to anyone. It is a reality that people may hurt, deceive, betray or even abandon you. Their actions are not your responsibility but you do have a role to play. Your primary role is to determine your own words, actions and lessons from each experience. You have the power to decide what hurts you or strengthens you. You choose whose voice holds influence in your life. You have the power to decide whether uninvited obstacles set you back or serve as inspiration to propel you forward with greater determination.

If you desire personal growth, commit to learning something new each day. To cultivate wisdom prioritize listening over speaking. If you seek a happy life, make small choices aligned with the things that bring you joy. If you want to receive love that matches the love you give, don't settle for just anyone; recognize your own value and appreciate the value in others. Understand that your happiness should never be compromised.

Settling for less doesn't indicate a lack of worth but rather a decision to not seek more. If you frequently find yourself running late, adjust your routine by going to bed earlier and waking up an hour earlier than usual. If financial security and a better life are your goals create a budget, practice wise stewardship and refrain from spending on unnecessary wants. Let go of the excuse of not having enough time; we all have the same 24 hours in a day. If others can accomplish their daily tasks, what is consuming your time?

There are countless daily excuses we use to justify negative outcomes but here's the truth: if you can identify someone leading the life you aspire to have, it's proof that what you think is impossible is truly achievable. If another person can find success, so can you! Mark Batterson, a Christian author, summarizes it perfectly: "If you're looking for an excuse, you will always find one. If you're looking for an opportunity, you will always discover one." As you begin to take responsibility for the outcomes in your life; your thoughts, actions, negotiations and social interactions will naturally shift.

Recognize that your success, health, love and well-being ultimately depend on you. What would you do differently if you truly embraced this concept? Now, question why you believe it doesn't apply to you. You must define your life's purpose and align your thoughts and actions accordingly. Hold yourself accountable for the results and setbacks you allow in your life. You are the CEO of your own life responsible for both the successes and challenges you encounter. Develop the habit of reflecting on your day, genuinely contemplating your thoughts and actions. Break it down into three areas for introspection:

Take a moment to reflect on your day and
consider the following questions:

1. What accomplishments or actions today do I feel I excelled at?

____

____

2. In what areas could I have improved or done better?

____

____

3. What circumstances or events were beyond my control and how will I choose to handle them?

____

____

4. What valuable lessons did I learn from these experiences?

____

____

By answering these questions honestly you can gain insights into your strengths, areas for growth and how to navigate situations that are outside of your control.

When you made the decision to purchase this book and you flipped that very first page you made a commitment to yourself to allow this content to confront you. The secret lies in the fact that you are now accountable for how you utilize and apply the insights that touch your heart. It's possible that upon finishing this book you may not see immediate results and that's perfectly alright. The truth is, a seed has been planted within you and only with the passage of time, dedicated effort and persistent action will its fruits be borne.

Self-awareness Questions

#INSURETHEACCOUNTABILITYBAG

1. When have you made another person responsible for your happiness or success?

____

____

2. Have you ever placed a burden on someone else's shoulder knowing it was your own weight to carry?

____

____

3. Do you lean more into making excuses instead of finding possibilities?

____

____

4. Make a list of the words and thoughts from yourself and others that you have allowed to dwell in your heart and have prevented you from moving towards a goal or dream.

____

____

5. Define your life tag and how you want people to quote you.

____

____

"I was once afraid of people saying,
"Who does she think she is?"

Now I have the courage to stand and
say, "This is who I am."

Oprah Winfrey

The Growth Bag

Indeed, growth is a fundamental aspect of human existence encompassing both physical and personal development. While the Oxford Dictionary defines growth as the process of increasing in physical size, it's important to note that growth extends beyond the physical realm. Personal growth, emotional maturity and intellectual development are equally significant aspects of human growth even though they may not always be as tangible or easily measurable as physical growth. Our journey through life involves continuous learning and improvement, contributing to our overall growth as individuals.

Personal growth encompasses a wide range of intangible aspects of our lives including our thoughts, reasoning, emotions and character. These areas are crucial indicators of our development as individuals. When we observe changes in how we react to situations, handle our emotions or make decisions based on a deeper understanding, it's a clear sign of personal growth. Emotional intelligence in particular, plays a significant role in our ability to navigate life's challenges with greater maturity and resilience. It's a testament to the ongoing evolution of our inner selves and our capacity for self-improvement.

A great analogy of growth can be seen like the developmental process of a photograph in a darkroom. Rushing or neglecting the necessary growth processes in our lives can indeed lead to unintended consequences or prevent us from reaching our full potential. Just as a photograph requires the right amount of time and care to reveal its true beauty in that of pictures and editing, personal growth is a unique and individualized journey that demands patience, effort and the right conditions.

Understanding that personal growth is a process, one that varies for each person and which allows us to appreciate the gradual transformation and development that leads to becoming the best version of ourselves. It's a reminder that success and self-improvement often go hand in hand with perseverance and a willingness to embrace the journey as a whole rather than rushing the process.

"Slow and steady wins the race," is a valuable philosophy to live by and it aligns with the idea that consistent effort and patience often lead to more lasting and meaningful achievements. Indeed, the journey of growth can be filled with challenges and moments of frustration but it's during this process that we acquire valuable experiences, skills and insights.

Falling in love with the journey of growth is a perspective that can make the path to achieving our goals more fulfilling and rewarding. It allows us to appreciate the small victories and lessons learned along the way, making the ultimate achievement all the more satisfying. This mindset encourages us to stay committed, resilient and focused on continuous improvement, which can ultimately lead to a more sustainable and enriching path to success.

My personal experience and perspective on challenges and hurdles have been truly insightful to say the least. Recognizing that challenges are an inherent part of life's journey and viewing them as opportunities for growth versus negative things that were happening to me, helped enrich a powerful mindset. Me approaching difficulties with the intention of extracting valuable lessons and insights from them really transformed my relationship with adversity.

By taking notes and actively seeking ways to learn and improve from each challenge you not only become more resilient but also turn adversity into a source of excitement and personal development. This shift in mindset can greatly enhance your ability to navigate life's ups and downs with grace and enthusiasm, ultimately leading to a more fulfilling and enriching life journey. It's a valuable lesson in itself, demonstrating the incredible power of perspective and personal growth.

Taking responsibility for your own self-growth and well-being is a fundamental aspect of personal development. It's essential to invest time and effort in yourself, make conscious decisions that benefit you and becoming self-aware to align your actions with your goals and values.

Choosing your social circle wisely is also crucial. Surrounding yourself with individuals who share your aspirations, ambition, and commitment to personal growth can be incredibly inspiring and moving. When you're in the company of people who are evolving and working towards their dreams, it can motivate you to do the same and create a positive ripple effect in your own life.

Ultimately, focusing on self-growth and choosing the right company can contribute significantly to your development and overall well-being.

The saying "your circle should stay small but your vision should stay big" underscores the idea that not everyone in your life at a given moment is meant to be a part of your long-term journey, especially if they hinder your personal growth or don't align with your goals and values.

As you evolve and pursue your vision of personal success and becoming the best version of yourself, it's essential to evaluate your relationships and ensure that they remain supportive and aligned with your aspirations. Standing firm in your alignment with your goals is crucial because, as you've noted, personal growth is a journey that requires time, effort and sometimes making difficult choices about who you surround yourself with to foster your development. It's about creating an environment that nurtures your growth and empowers you to achieve your full potential.

And while it's admirable to help others in their journey, it's essential to maintain boundaries and not let their struggles or negativity hinder you. The idea of not allowing others to bring you into their darkness but instead bringing them into your light is a powerful reminder of the importance of maintaining a positive and uplifting perspective.

Sometimes despite your best efforts, you may not be able to bring someone into your light, and in such cases, it's wise to prioritize your own growth and well-being. Moving on and continuing to shine bright is a testament to your resilience and commitment to your own personal journey. It's a valuable lesson in self-care and self-preservation while still extending a helping hand when you can.

If you're lucky enough to finally feel free and comfortable with those around you, your tribe it's crucial to be intentional and invest time and effort into nurturing those relationships with family, friends, romantic partners, colleagues and acquaintances. The quote by Robert Ransom emphasizes the idea that relationships, like personal growth, require labor and patience before reaping the rewards of connection and joy.

Balancing self-development with the cultivation of relationships is indeed important. Isolating oneself entirely can lead to loneliness and a lack of support when needed, while overly prioritizing others can result in neglecting one's own identity.

Choosing the right individuals to accompany you on your journey of growth is a thoughtful process. Building a supportive and balanced network of relationships can provide not only companionship but also valuable support and celebration when you reach your goals. Your perspective highlights the significance of finding the right balance in life where both self-growth and meaningful connections thrive together.

Achieving a balance between personal growth and your relationships can indeed provide greater clarity, consciousness and efficiency in various aspects of life, including wealth, career and investments. When you strike that balance, you're better equipped to work smarter and make informed decisions utilizing the systems and opportunities in your favor.

The pursuit of milestones is a commendable approach to personal and professional development. Milestones represent significant achievements that go beyond mere success; they mark important points of progress and personal growth. They serve as tangible evidence of your journey and the value you've created along the way. Striving for milestones can be a powerful motivator on your path towards achieving your goals and becoming the best version of yourself.

What constitutes growth or success can vary greatly from one person to another and it's essential for each individual to define these terms based on their own values, aspirations and unique path.

Recognizing and celebrating both the little wins and the significant milestones is a wise approach. The small victories along the way are just as important as the major achievements, as they reflect progress and effort. Acknowledging these incremental steps can provide motivation and a sense of accomplishment throughout your personal journey. Ultimately, the definition of success and growth should be deeply personal and reflective of you, your ambitions and journey along the way.

Just like a baby's first steps are celebrated and seen as a crucial part of the learning process, the incremental progress and practice in any endeavor should be acknowledged and appreciated just the same.

If I can reference sales skills and understanding people's different personalities as an example in many aspects of life, including personal and professional interactions, having a good grasp of human psychology and interpersonal dynamics can be immensely valuable. It allows you to navigate relationships and situations with greater empathy, adaptability and effectiveness, ultimately contributing to your success.

Coming into real estate the very first company that I hung my license with, lead with personality tests. What was it about the personality test that was so efficient?

Personality tests and assessments can be highly important tools, especially in fields like real estate and sales, where understanding and connecting with people is paramount. Here's why they are valuable:

1. **Personalized Approach** Personality tests provide insights into an individual's preferences, strengths, weaknesses and communication styles. This information allows companies to tailor their training, support and resources to suit the individual's needs.

2. **Client Understanding** Knowing your own personality traits and those of your clients can be invaluable. It helps in building rapport, adapting your approach and anticipating client needs effectively. Different clients may respond better to distinct communication styles and strategies.

3. **Motivation and Self-Awareness** Personality assessments can help individuals understand their intrinsic motivators and areas where they might need improvement. This self-awareness can guide personal development efforts and lead to more effective goal setting.

4. **Team Dynamics** In a team environment, understanding the diverse personalities within the team can enhance collaboration. It helps team members appreciate each other's strengths and contributions, leading to better teamwork and outcomes.

> 5. **Reducing Stagnation** As mentioned, people have different levels of motivation and growth trajectories. Personality assessments can shed light on what drives individuals and how they can maintain or increase their motivation for continuous improvement.

In summary, personality tests can be helpful towards fostering personal and professional growth, enhancing communication and optimizing performance in various fields. They provide a framework for understanding and leveraging individual differences to achieve greater success.

To give an example, the personality or DISC test breaks personalities down in letter form consisting of I, S, C, D personalities and sometimes just personality traits. In the test I took on 16personalities.com, I was described as the following and I'll tell you how it relates to me understanding how I should grow as a person:

The test result mentioned that I was:

61% Extroverted- Extroverted individuals readily enjoy group activities and value social interaction. They tend to be outwardly enthusiastic and express their excitement.

Therefore, I have a great chance of experiencing motivation and growth through networking events where I can meet new people and collaborate. These are the things that are my natural make up. The entire idea of this is to help you understand how you can move through life in your truest form and be successful while doing it.

72% Intuitive- Intuitive individuals are very imaginative, open-minded and curious. They value originality and focus on hidden meanings and distant possibilities. Being an intuitive individual helps me in life and career growth because I'm able to use my intuition to understand things for what they are and it creates a natural empathy for people and situations helping me connect like a charm.

73% Feeler vs Thinker- Feeling individuals value emotional expression and sensitivity. They place a lot of importance on empathy, social harmony and cooperation. Although I beg to differ slightly, because I'm a very deep and analytical thinker. However, the "feeler" could in large part, comprise my ability to be a deep feeler first.

My ability to understand and leverage insights about my own personality as well as those of others, has been a significant asset in both my personal and professional journey. It's a testament to the power of self-awareness and emotional intelligence.

By recognizing your own traits, strengths and areas for improvement you can make informed decisions and set realistic goals for self-advancement. Additionally, understanding the personalities of others allows you to adapt your communication style, build rapport and create more harmonious and mutually beneficial relationships which can be especially beneficial in a client-oriented profession like mine.

My approach of cultivating intentional relationships with clients based on mutual understanding has not only been effective but also demonstrates a high level of professionalism and empathy on my part. It's a valuable skill that has led to long-lasting and successful partnerships.

Self-Awareness Questions

#INSURETHEGROWTHBAG

1. Do you celebrate the small wins to inspire continuous growth?

____

____

2. Try measuring your growth in intervals, i.e. every 5 years, each month, etc.

____

____

3. How does your growth compare to those surrounding you?

____

____

4. Think about when hard times have led to extreme growing moments.

____

____

5. Do you feel the relationships you are cultivating have mutual benefits?

____

____

"The comfort zone is a psychological
state in which one feels familiar, safe,
at ease, and secure.

If you always do what is easy and
choose the path of least resistance,
you never step outside your comfort
zone. Great things don't come from
comfort zones."

Roy T. Bennett

The Sustainability Bag

When we hear the word sustainability, we immediately think about the basic concept of staying afloat. What sustainability means is to take the necessary measures today to fulfill the needs of our current generation, in order to ensure the needs of future generations. Investing in sustainability for yourself is a wise and forward-thinking decision.

I want to share with you four areas in which you should pay close attention when making the decision to invest in your personal sustainability; these are both my experiences and how they have shaped my life.

It's a common tendency for many people to prioritize the needs of others over their own but neglecting one's own well-being can have long-term consequences. Don't get me wrong, serving others is a gift from God and a beautiful act of love, BUT...

It is essential to find a balance between serving others and taking care of yourself. By continuously putting off your own needs, desires and goals, you may reach a point where it becomes more challenging to achieve them. This emphasizes the importance of self-care and self-prioritization to ensure a better future for yourself and those around you.

I personally think focusing predominantly on sources outside of yourself and your business are simply called distractions.

Distractions especially those that divert your time and attention away from your priorities, can indeed have a significant impact on your ability to achieve your desired outcomes.

While also recognizing that nobody is immune to distractions and imperfections, I still place deep emphasis on maintaining tunnel vision as the main priority when adhering to your core values, objectives and goals. Time is a finite resource and using it wisely to pursue your own aspirations is a key to personal sustainability and fulfillment.

One of the things I pride myself in is being able to block out all the noise and hone in on my goals. I call it "beast mode," and I swear in those moments nothing and no one can deter me from what I'm scheduled to achieve. I simply will not allow it! I get really upset with distractions and delays that I go even harder to make up for lost time!

Striking a balance between addressing external demands and staying true to your own path is an ongoing challenge but one if followed, can lead to a more purposeful and successful life. How quickly our end goals can be shattered by losing focus is a valuable reminder that maintaining focus on what truly matters is and will always be the key.

It's a common human tendency to use distractions as a means to avoid facing reality, seeking temporary relief from problems or challenges; however, these issues don't disappear and often become more daunting when ignored.

Confronting reality and addressing responsibilities directly is indeed a more effective and empowered approach. It allows you to tackle each issue as it arises leading to more favorable outcomes. Having faith in oneself and one's abilities is crucial. Believing in your capacity to overcome challenges and accomplish your goals can shift your mindset towards focusing on solutions rather than distractions.

Ultimately, this perspective should encourage you to develop resilience, confront challenges head-on, and cultivate a sense of self-belief that leads to a more focused and empowered approach to life's ebbs and flows.

In a world filled with external influences and opinions, it's easy to lose sight of who you are and what you truly value.

Maintaining a sense of self and staying grounded is essential. While feedback and guidance from others can be valuable, it's crucial to distinguish between constructive input and external pressures that may lead you away from your authentic self.

Having a clear understanding of your convictions and non-negotiables in life provides a strong foundation for making decisions and staying true to your values. This self-awareness and self-assuredness make you less susceptible to being swayed by every external voice and opinion. No one person's voice in your life should be louder than your own.

Which brings me to the second area you should pay close attention to when investing in yourself: sustaining you!

Just to give you a little of my family backstory, my mother was one of 11 children, but still managed to take her life to higher heights despite the neighborhood or challenging upbringing she experienced. Born and raised in Jersey City, she took jobs in different fields cities and states, traveled the world with her two daughters and husband bravely, with no family around. My stepfather was in the military and did numerous tours in Afghanistan, Iraq, Kuwait, Korea, Japan, just to name a few; and plenty of times my mom as a result of his career obligations and outside of financial was forced to hold it down, in foreign places, the majority of the time raising her two girls on her own. As a woman now, I always think about the emotional toll it must've taken on her to be so far away from your huge family, not knowing if your husband will come home dead or alive when he goes away to war and still having to do cheerleading and gymnastic practices, help with homework, cute birthday parties and sleepovers for your girls, manage a successful real estate career, etc. Despite all of that some of her family back home in Jersey City just saw her as a success, with two daughters who were also destined for the same.

On my father's side, my Dad grew up completely different. Born in NYC went to private school and was born to two successful parents, one a wealthy insurance professional and the other a super successful realtor. My grandfather started his long-standing career in insurance dating back to the late 70s as a corporate leader of a life insurance company, prior to opening an insurance agency in Manhattan in 1986. My Nana was a super successful realtor out of Hoboken, NJ and a part of the millionaire's club when brownstones were selling for $25k. My father went off to get into the insurance and mortgage business, amongst other things. To my father's side of the family, I was once again destined for success according to everyone.

So basically I spent all of my life sustaining "them." Sustaining what my parents and grandparents told me I would be. Sustaining aunts and uncle's ideas on who I would be as well as cousins, thought processes of who they "knew" I would be. All of this took a mental toll on me for a very long time; it's like I couldn't find myself in everyone else's opinion of my life. Then eventually the whole family, parents and grandparents included, found out that I wanted to be everything- LOL. A teacher sent a letter to my mom saying "In class today, Ashley stated that she wanted to be a lawyer by day and DJ by night." That was so funny explaining to her the logic in that, but then I told my dad and grandfather that I wanted to be an actress and a professional cheerleader. My grandfather insured a lot of influential people and had a client and friend who was a producer of the show "Law & Order," and let me check the set out one day. It was a pretty cool experience and I still want to be an actress- LOL.

I've been writing since I was 9 short stories, poems, song lyrics, etc. and knew that I was a writer but I had decided very early on that I wasn't interested in doing it for a career. Although my mom fought me tooth and nail until I ended up in college for Journalism. Finally, I loved my creative vision and eye for home fashions and just knew that I wanted to be an interior designer, so off to the Art Institute I went to get a degree in Interior Design but at the same time declining a paid internship at Ethan Allen. Make it make sense.

My immediate family became very frustrated with all of my indecisions, which made me feel like a disappointment. However, at some point in my 20s I decided to unapologet-ically, (because I had already been going by the beat of my own drum since I could walk probably) but I unapologeti-cally this time, decided to live life on my own terms and who-ever didn't like it, oh well. Eventually, I decided to follow in my family's footsteps and become a realtor first and insur-ance agent afterwards. Doing things my way, prioritizing myself first and sustaining me was low key turning me into a rebel without a cause.

When I obtained my real estate license at 20, my mom was one of the owners of the real estate company so I walked around like I owned the place. The moment of clarity was my mom walking in on me and my friend having lunch in her office. This lunch consisted of Mexican food and Coronas. My explanation to my mom, "we would have a beer if we ate at the restaurant, so we did the same when we took it to go." She literally had to teach me professional etiquette and set me straight though, I'm sure I don't need to go into detail.

I got my insurance license at 23 and started working at my family's agency. My Grandfather really pissed me off when he insinuated that I couldn't put the white fur rug by my desk. I told him that he just didn't understand that the way a place is decorated determines the Feng Shui; that didn't go well either and he too let me have it. In these moments, I realized that sustaining myself and not others, was not a reason to be obnoxiously self-indulged and inconsiderate of others' opinions and ways of thinking. "Sustaining you" was more of internally believing and valuing your own ideas, decisions and desires within reason while helping others understand that regardless of their agreement, it doesn't provide the right to frown upon and undermine your visions. And that doesn't mitigate the severity in which you consider their opinions.

Essentially, you don't want to have a God complex and become your own worst enemy but you also don't want to constantly be at the mercy of others. Maintaining humility by acknowledging that none of us knows everything is crucial. It's in the blend of our collective knowledge and experiences that often lies the best path forward.

Balancing the mind and achieving emotional equilibrium is indeed a worthy goal. It allows you to make informed decisions, consider multiple viewpoints and navigate life's complexities with greater wisdom and resilience. Striking this balance helped me foster healthy relationships and encouraged both self-assurance and a willingness to learn from others.

On the flip-side and to my defense, (I'm still working on being less defensive by the way) the whole time I just looked at things similar to that of the biblical principle "love thy neighbor as you do yourself." It highlights the notion that taking care of oneself is not a selfish act but rather a fundamental aspect of being able to love and serve others effectively. Pretty much if I wasn't happy with the path of my life, how in the world would I have made my family happy?

However, there is a such thing in any relationship, even friendships, where when you carve out time for self-care and make decisions that put your well-being first, it may indeed lead to negative reactions from those who were accustomed to your constant availability or your way of being that they were comfortable with. Some might label it as selfishness but as aptly pointed out, it's about achieving a healthier balance that would allow me to serve others more authentically and effectively.

Regardless, two things can be true and self-care is not only acceptable but also essential.

This second factor goes hand in hand with the third area of recommendation; sustaining your body, mind and soul, as it enables you to operate at your best and contribute positively to the lives of others.

I had seemed to have mastered the sustainability of my mind, knowing exactly what I wanted in life, but being proud of the idea of always evolving and still rolling with the punches, my punches. However, the body and soul I would realize years later was so drastically neglected, making it nearly impossible to be in one accord with myself. Becoming an entrepreneur at such an early age toyed with my entire state of being. I mean there were financial woes, lack of confidence at times due to my age and people not taking me seriously and old habits of inconsistency with dedication to any one goal or project. Due to all of my mental and emotional struggles I gained so much weight than I had ever in my life, due to bad relationships, etc. I became so far removed from my true-blue self. They were some of the most miserable years of my existence and made me so unaligned with all things me.

I had to have a come to Jesus moment with myself and keep it real about who I was as a person, who I was becoming and how did it get this far? In this moment, I had to think back to my early years and how creative, free flowing, spontaneous and brave I had always been. What happened I asked myself, then I realized that the boyfriend happened, the party life happened, the low account balance happened. Literally everything, in my eyes, happened except the reality that I had let myself go. That's when I understood that I had been the first one to let someone else know the ways in which they've disappointed me but yet I was now doing the very same thing to myself. In times of despair, I always think back to me as a kid saying "when I'm 18 I'll be an adult and in control of my own destiny and no one can tell me what to do anymore. My life will be what I make it." That's when the reality check always hits like okay little girl, is this the life that you wanted so badly to make? Does it make you proud or no?

I was finally understanding that true well-being requires attention to all aspects of my being.

Taking care of your body through proper nutrition, rest and medical checkups is foundational. Without good health it becomes challenging to pursue your goals and enjoy life to the fullest.

Sustaining your mind involves practices like mindfulness which can help manage stress and anxiety, enhance focus and improve decision-making. Mindfulness and other mental well-being practices are essential in today's fast-paced and stressful world.

Nurturing your soul goes beyond merely depending solely on your specific faith or belief system, even God only helps those "who help themselves." It's about finding practices or experiences that connect you with a sense of inner peace, purpose and contentment.

When I decided to take my health and wellness more seriously I immediately hired a trainer. Some may hire a personal trainer because they feel they just need help losing weight or gaining muscle, etc. I did it because I knew that I was almost never consistent in the gym beyond 3 months max. I would lose 10 lbs and stop because it would happen so quickly. Until it wasn't happening so quickly anymore and I now had to watch what I ate because age and body maturity was getting the best of me. I knew that I would stay on this fitness journey if I had a scheduled time to be at the gym 3x a week and my money was invested so now I put myself in an uncomfortable and compromising position to follow through (outside of my comfort zone). I was challenging all of my past transgressions the inconsistencies and the idea that I could just move on and start something else, do things on my own time in my comfort zone, etc. At the gym none of those things were an option, I realized. If I didn't do the exercises what were the other options to burn fat and build muscle, nothing. If I didn't feel like doing the work out at all while at the gym, what was the other option, again nothing. I was in an uphill battle with my old self and the new and improved me that I wanted to prove I could be. With that, I stuck it out with multiple trainers, I guess I still had to find a way to be inconsistent. Rome wasn't built in a day, LOL I'm still working on myself; regardless, I stayed consistent for not just 3 months anymore but nearly 2 years. This experience was so imperative in my journey because I had finally shown myself what following through to completion looked like ,it was invigorating and taught me so much about myself and my potential in all facets of my life.

Which perfectly leads to my last point sustaining what you obtain. After spending thousands on personal training and my dedication to maintaining my physical health over the past two years, my mental well-being and my business success despite a busy schedule underscored the idea that coming this far is not an endpoint but a stepping stone to further growth in my life.

There is a famous Benjamin Franklin quote that says: *"when the well is dry, we know the worth of water."* This quote is a poignant reminder of the significance of proactive measures in sustaining what we value. Whether it's our health, our achievements or our personal relationships, taking steps to protect and maintain them is imperative.

Don't wait to reach the point that you lose things you have worked very hard for by not taking the necessary measure to sustain, keep and value them. This happens to be a topic I am so fluent in as I own an insurance agency; where highlighting the value of planning and preparation for unexpected challenges is a part of my professional teachings.

Indeed, personal sustainability involves making choices and taking actions.

So make a plan to take the necessary steps to take personal sustainability seriously and love yourself a bit more along the way.

Self-Awareness Questions

1. What are ways that you can sustain your mind, body and soul?

   ____

   ____

2. Think back to activities from your youth; that's your happy place.

   ____

   ____

3. Who were you before the world shifted your point of view?

   ____

   ____

4. Mental health is so pivotal in sustaining you; how are you taking care of that daily?

   ____

   ____

"I am only one, but I am one. I cannot
do everything, but I can do something. And I will not let what I cannot
do interfere with what I can do."

– Edward Everett Hale

The Love Bag

Some souls are destined to collide
but not always destined to be.

At this moment, the timing couldn't have been more opportune to write this book. Throughout this phase of my life I've undergone numerous transitions helping my understanding of both myself and any romantic partner. By "partner," I don't solely refer to an official spouse but rather anyone with whom you share any level of romantic connection, be it spiritual or physical. This journey has allowed me to discern between love, lust and the various idiosyncratic ways people express affection. I've come to realize that love isn't always mirrored or reciprocated in the same manner by each individual but only as each person individually knows how to show it.

Yet, another lesson I've grasped is that love doesn't always adhere to a script; at times, it arrives unexpectedly on your doorstep as it is, not necessarily conforming to your idealized expectations. It's crucial to consider the timing when love enters your life: is it there for a particular reason, merely for a passing phase or perhaps as a lifelong blessing?

With that being said, just because love can sometimes be temporary rather than the permanency we've all grown to hope for, it always serves the purpose of learning new ways to love and new ways of love.

Understanding the nuances of love and recognizing that each relationship is unique with its own dynamics and boundaries, is an important aspect of navigating the complexities of human connection. It focuses on the importance of communication, empathy and mutual respect in all types of relationships.

Regardless of the outcome, love is a deeply personal and evolving experience and it's worth embracing the various dimensions and lessons it offers in our lives.

In romantic relationships, the depth of that love may only be understood by the two, hence keeping outside influences at bay whom might not be able to fully understand, feel or see the depths of that love and what two beings share.

Love indeed encompasses a range of emotions and experiences that can vary in depth and nature. I'm now understanding that love is not as unconditional as I once knew it to be but actually very conditional in the same. Before I break down what I mean I would just like to add that I am very specifically referencing, love in romantic relationships, friendships, family, love for yourself and love for all that you are.

Unconditional love most associated with love for family, implies a deep and enduring connection that transcends circumstances and flaws. It's a love that remains steadfast even in the face of challenges; this love can also be found in very close friendships and soul mates.

On the other hand, conditional love acknowledges that boundaries and expectations exist in relationships.

Encompassing that while love may be strong it can still be affected by actions, choices and behaviors that impact the quality of the connection.

While unconditional love embraces you regardless of circumstances, conditional love necessitates meeting certain standards to transform into unconditional love. This type of love often challenges you to become stronger, improve, alter habits and adjust your lifestyle and mindset. This can sometimes lead one to question whether genuine love should demand changes in appearance, income, or physical body, fostering uncertainty about the authenticity of the affection.

Conditional love can be seen as a form of love that challenges and encourages personal growth and improvement, the one that keeps you on your toes. It recognizes that people have areas for development and change and encourages them to reach their fullest potential instead of sacrificing one's self in the name of love; because while you love them, you love yourself just as much to only accept the best form of love.

In this context, conditional love isn't about rejecting someone for who they are but rather about encouraging their journey toward becoming the best version of themselves. It's a direct reflection of the care and admiration you have for your own self and your life 's desires.

Balancing this desire for personal growth and improvement with acceptance and love for someone as they are presently versus the potential of what you personally expect and want can be a delicate but valuable aspect of relationships. It acknowledges that love is not stagnant but can be a force for positive change and transformation, if handled both carefully and in a healthy manner.

Love can be a powerful catalyst for personal development and a source of deep fulfillment if all parties are willing to both acknowledge it, cultivate, nurture and grow it as they normally would in other aspects of their life.

And in the mist of us strongly desiring the love we all feel we deserve, whether that be the love of our lives romantically, a better love between our family members, the ultimate friend group that feels just like family and the like, while having faith, daily prayers and keeping God's plan at the forefront is pivotal in ensuring this happens.

It's common for individuals to have specific expectations and ideas of how their prayers should be answered and sometimes these preconceptions can lead to difficulties in recognizing the answers that have come, though in unexpected forms.

Faith involves surrendering to a higher will and allowing divine guidance to shape your life. It's about trust, patience and accepting that the path may not always align with your own plans and desires. It's a recognition that God's will may sometimes lead you in directions you hadn't envisioned but ultimately serves your highest good.

In the process of letting God's will be done in your life, having genuine faith and surrendering control allowing room for divine intervention and guidance in your life cannot be ignored. It's a reminder that faith isn't about enforcing your own will but about aligning with a higher purpose and trusting in the wisdom of a greater plan.

My personal experience with faith and prayer beautifully coincides with the concept of divine timing and the idea that what we ask for may be granted in a way that aligns with a higher plan, rather than our immediate expectations.

The analogy of receiving something in increments like money for example, to prevent squandering, suggests that sometimes, what we desire or pray for needs to be received gradually to allow for personal growth, appreciation and readiness to handle the blessings in our lives once received. For if we were to receive them prematurely like money, we may squander it.

The journey of faith often involves patience, trust and the recognition that divine timing is always at play and its purpose surpassing far more than you could imagine. Always remember that your openness to patiently receiving love and blessings in unexpected forms and during times least expected, is a testament to your faith and wisdom. Faith without works is dead!

Very specifically my prayer was to never lose myself again in a relationship. At the same time God was saying in order to not lose yourself you first need to work on yourself.

Part of God's answered prayer was telling me to work on myself in all aspects of life, including income, health, cultivating better relationships with others and understanding my own past and traumas. These were all crucial components and prerequisites of him allowing me to build a foundation for a successful and fulfilling love to come, God's handpicked choice for me!

His advice felt similarly to "stay ready, so you don't have to get ready." Understanding this helped me to not focus on a particular man but more importantly instead, the ongoing self-improvement and self-awareness required to ensure that I would be well-prepared to embrace the love and blessings coming my way.

Taking the time to get to know yourself, embracing your quirks, strengths and vulnerabilities and nurturing a deep understanding of who you are is so necessary.

When you love and value yourself, you approach relationships from a place of strength and authenticity. You bring your full self to the table which fosters genuine connections built on trust and mutual respect.

While I feel I've put in a lot of self-work to become who I am thus far, I do understand that personal growth is an ongoing journey and that there's always more to learn as you continue to grow in age and experience. I can humbly admit that these things are lifelong endeavors no matter what.

Understanding how you show up in the world these are all things that you need to ultimately be proud of, be at peace with and have full-blown understanding of just exactly how you operate so that when you go out into the world to collaborate with others such as, friends or any other relationships you have a full understanding of yourself and your ultimate value add.

Seeing all these things in yourself will help you best clearly see them in others hence, removing any worry or concern on how others perceive you and your perceptions, but instead providing full confidence in your decisions and how you see and deal with others. This is something very important that will help you in romantic love, because being one with yourself and having confidence is a top ingredient of any relationship. Once you get into a relationship with someone, you want to be confident in all of your abilities and confident in that person and the choice that you made to be with them. Even if that person is not fully confident in themselves, your confidence and the love that you two share will ultimately conquer all and that's what unconditional-conditional love is all about.

***There is one type of love that you can insure without the fear of it being a bad investment: self-love.

I am aware there may be many books, podcasts and diverse resources that speak on the importance of self-love and although this may not be my specific area of expertise, I am a witness based on personal experience on how loving and accepting yourself can be a game changer. When reflecting on "insuring the love bag," there are three critical aspects that come to mind:

1) Loving you regarding self-care and self-love

2) Loving others – acceptance and treatment

3) Loving life – gratitude, hope, and optimism

When discussing self-love, my focus extends beyond the conventional message of accepting oneself or seeing oneself through the lens of God's perspective. While these aspects are crucial, I place greater emphasis on perceiving beauty amidst shitty situations, recognizing strength in moments of turmoil and discovering radiance within darkness. To me, self-love involves delving deeper to understand the distinction between selfishness and selflessness. The term "selfish" often carries a negative connotation, whereas "self-less" is regarded as positive. There's truth in both perspectives; however, constantly prioritizing others' needs at the expense of your own without addressing your own well-being, can lead to a dangerous lifestyle.

When we label someone as selfish, the assumption often revolves around their lack of consideration for others. Conversely, being selfless can sometimes imply minimal or no concern for oneself. Here lies the complexity: you cannot offer others what you don't possess yourself. While self-lessness is commonly praised and promoted as a virtue, if it dominates the way you love yourself and live your life you may consistently place yourself last. There come moments in life when prioritizing yourself is imperative. You need to become your top supporter, allowing for personal time to enhance self-preservation for opportunities such as securing a job or relationship. Assisting others holds beauty as discussed earlier, but it's equally vital to prioritize self-care an essential aspect of self-love.

By practicing this you'll begin to acknowledge love within yourself, perceiving it as you do in others. You'll strive for wellness seeking to maintain a balanced and healthy life. Grant yourself permission to embrace both the positive and negative aspects of your life. It's essential to allow yourself moments of enjoyment and pursue pleasure without feeling guilty. Similarly, you must permit yourself to navigate through the emotions and cycles that accompany setbacks in any aspect of life. It's inevitable to stumble or make mistakes to choose wrongly and potentially hurt both yourself and others along the way. Grant yourself the freedom not to pursue perfection.

Believing that being a perfectionist is a virtue rather than a flaw burdens oneself with an unnecessary weight. Our purpose isn't to attain perfection, as it's unattainable. Rather, our aim is to commit to excellence in all we do, based on our abilities and available resources. It's alright to not feel okay; however, it's important not to linger in that mental or emotional state for too long. Grant yourself forgiveness! Sometimes it's simpler to forgive others than it is to forgive ourselves for mistakes or past decisions, engaging in mental debates of "what if" or "I should have." These inner conflicts can impede your progress. Allow yourself a break and show compassion to your soul; this too is an act of self-love.

In the realm of loving others, acknowledging the treatment you accept from them and the acceptance of yourself is crucial. Once you've mastered self-love in its true essence, you recognize that the way you treat others mirrors how you perceive yourself. Value yourself enough to surround yourself with those who bring genuine joy, contribute positively to your life and support your seemingly wild dreams. Have the courage to distance yourself from individuals who disrupt your inner peace. Not everyone in your circle radiates positive energy toward you or in general. Surrounding yourself with the right people becomes a significant aspect of self-love. The individuals you allow into your life will influence it and the voice within it. Consequently, it's important not to internalize others' opinions about yourself. Granting others, a voice in your life is significant hence the need for careful selection and recognition of this privilege.

While we often allow individuals in our close circle who share similar traits or interests, the reality is that despite apparent similarities we're all navigating different life paths. Hence, it's crucial to grant yourself permission to experience both the positive and negative aspects of life and to accept that making mistakes is a part of learning and growth—they serve as our most profound lessons. Embrace self-forgiveness and avoid carrying unnecessary burdens. Lastly, prioritize self-love to ensure that your own voice remains the strongest among all those surrounding you.

As we conclude this chapter on insuring the love bag, it's crucial to underscore the significance of embracing life with a sense of gratitude, hope and optimism. Cultivate an attitude of appreciation for both present blessings and future possibilities. At times, we become so absorbed in pursuing what we desire that we overlook the value of what we already possess. This undermines the need for optimism on what we focus on expands whether positive or negative. Hence, fostering an optimistic outlook and maintaining hope while embracing life to its fullest extent is an integral part of insuring the love bag.

Allow me to share this last point with you: the pivotal moment I made a conscious choice to cultivate a meaningful relationship with God acknowledging all He does and the opportunities He grants, I began to truly value Him for affording me another chance at life. When you genuinely love someone, you consider their importance. Because my devotion to God runs deep, I felt remorseful for neglecting Him, taking for granted the breath He bestowed upon me and squandering time without living up to the potential He envisioned for me. Consequently every night, I leave my blinds partially open, ensuring that each morning I awaken to the radiant brilliance of the sun piercing through the clouds. This daily spectacle serves as a constant reminder of His boundless grace towards me and His unwavering belief that I merit another day to make amends, pursue my aspirations and more. This unparalleled kind of love stands as a steadfast force that never abandons or disappoints.

Self-Awareness Questions

1. What defines love to you?

2. We give a lot of thought into how others love us but how do you love others?

3. Do you wake up every morning with a sense of gratitude for being given another chance at life?

4. What experiences in your life contribute to the way that you love?

"The greatest happiness of life is the conviction that we are loved; loved for ourselves, or rather, loved in spite of ourselves."

–Victor Hugo

The Difficult Bag

- Identifying and not internalizing challenges

Identifying versus internalizing.

By definition, identifying is to establish or indicate who or what (someone or something) is. While internalizing is defined as make attitudes or behavior part of one's nature by learning.

In essence, recognizing challenges without internalizing them involves understanding their origins or causes without allowing them to define our core identity. Throughout life, we encounter various difficulties that we sometimes assimilate into our sense of self. For instance, growing up in foster care might lead one to feel like an orphan, unloved and unwanted. However, the reality could be that you were simply a child removed from a home due to circumstances like the loss of a parent or inadequate familial support, among other reasons. Similarly, events in our past may shape our character and it's easy to attribute who we are solely to those experiences. Yet it's crucial not to let these events become the entire narrative of our lives.

Life, uniquely ours, allows us to transform and align it with who and what we aspire to become regardless of past or present experiences. It's crucial not to internalize challenges as doing so can steer us towards a precarious path.

By adopting a more positive outlook, we fulfill the essence of recognizing challenges without assimilating them into our identity. This entails comprehending the origin, nature, timing and circumstances surrounding a problem without taking personal blame acknowledging that the issue may not have arisen solely due to our actions or faults.

Mastering this approach requires extensive learning and training to focus on positive outcomes. By engaging in what I refer to as "positive outcome training," it involves dissecting negative situations to uncover the hidden benefits. This involves courage and optimism allowing us to anticipate a positive future outcome even when uncertain about the specifics. This optimistic outlook enables us to maintain hope envisioning a favorable outcome that propels us in the right direction. Instead of perceiving a challenging moment as entirely detrimental, we embrace it as a learning experience acknowledging its potential for growth despite its immediate emotional impact.

When we refrain from internalizing it, we're refraining from bearing the weighty burden that it imposes on our lives. This approach enables us to maintain hope and see the possibilities ahead. Instead, we opt to acknowledge and identify the issue, allowing us to question its relevance in our lives. Personally, adopting this mindset has assisted me in releasing and unpacking burdens that were never mine to carry in the first place. Often, we shoulder the burdens and struggles of those around us—be it parents, grandparents, friends, coworkers or bosses. However, many of these issues may not directly impact our future or may not affect us personally at all. We've learned to adopt these burdens out of compassion or a lack of alternative perspectives.

Mastering the tactic of asking, "is this truly a me problem?" is a powerful approach. For instance, if your partner makes objective comments about the opposite gender which incidentally includes you, the immediate reaction might be to take it personally viewing it as an attack on your identity as a man or woman. However, upon reflection, you might question the relevance of such comments to yourself. For instance, as a woman, if the discussion revolves around stereotypes of using men for wealth or marriage and you don't fit that description it becomes clearer that it's not a reflection of your character. Similarly, if there's a widespread belief that "all men cheat," but you are a faithful and committed individual this stereotype wouldn't perturb you as it doesn't align with your personal values and conduct.

Comprehending why external comments or experiences affect us, especially when they contradict our true character or the perception others have of us, boils down to the concept of empathy and compassion.

Having compassion is a valuable trait as it enables you to empathize with others' emotions and concerns, even when you haven't directly experienced them yourself. However, it can turn negative if it's used as a manipulative tool to make you believe that everyone or everything similar to your situation is identical. What I've just accomplished is recognizing an issue without internalizing it. By choosing not to internalize it, we can redirect it back to the source and offer support or words of comfort to aid them in dealing with the particular situation that's causing distress. Through this approach, we maintain our own inner peace while potentially assisting someone else in finding theirs. This situation isn't my personal burden and it never was, but I'm willing to help you navigate why it's affecting you to find a resolution.

Consider that adopting the perspective that a problem doesn't belong to you but to the individual attempting to impose it upon you can trigger a ripple effect of emotions. This underscores the importance of discerning the variations in perception that influence our interactions with others, particularly in specific situations. Some individuals tend to assume a victim mentality where they may perceive something as their problem even when it's not, foreseeing it becoming an issue for them. These individuals often approach situations from a negative standpoint. Consequently, we have the choice to either involve ourselves or distance ourselves from the individual, the situation or the topic, whether momentarily or entirely, based on these observations.

While we've covered a few instances illustrating the process of recognizing and internalizing challenges, there exist countless other examples that echo the same sentiment. Regardless of the topic chosen to substantiate this assertion, the key lies in discerning both the positive and negative aspects within them. This concept circles back to the power of positive thinking. The belief that "you can" leads to accomplishment, while the doubt inherent in "trying" implies a potential failure. Employing the term "try" suggests making an attempt without ensuring success. If we navigate life with this mindset, constantly assuming that things may or may not work out, it impedes our ability to reach the pinnacle of success in relationships, business endeavors, financial pursuits and even our personal well-being.

Hence when confronted with any adverse situation, acquiring the skill of pivoting becomes crucial. Mastering the art of pivoting stands as an essential skill set indispensable for achieving success. The harsh reality remains that despite nurturing numerous positive thoughts, circumstances can veer off course not aligning with our initial hopes. This is precisely where pivoting enters the scene. When we pivot, we acknowledge that while our initial approach might not have succeeded there are alternative ways or individuals with whom success can still be achieved. It's about recognizing that though one avenue may not have worked there are other routes or different collaborators that can lead to the desired outcome.

- Finding solutions

One aspect that I take immense pride in is my inclination towards finding solutions. Delving into this topic excites me more than anything else in this book. If I could inhabit a world where everyone solely focused on solutions, it would truly be a paradise for me. I chose to adopt a solution-oriented mindset simply because it avoids unnecessary complications. While many can pinpoint problems, I believe only a few can genuinely uncover the solutions to those problems. Although some have labeled me as a complainer, I'd argue that I'm more someone who becomes frustrated when the reasons behind issues aren't explored.

To keep it concise, my main concern is determining whether an issue can be resolved and if possible, what steps are necessary for its resolution. The path to finding a solution begins by outlining the initial step toward resolution and continues from there. We've already progressed past the stage of recognizing and not internalizing issues. Now that we've pinpointed the problem the next question is how to remedy it. If the issue proves unfixable the best approach involves directly confronting it or, if feasible, removing oneself entirely from the situation. I acknowledge that some individuals simply resist finding solutions often preferring to linger on a problem. Exploring why certain individuals or groups opt to dwell on issues rather than seeking resolutions to promote collective happiness is a topic worth exploring, rooted in the idea that misery tends to seek company.

If you're not seeking answers, you're merely fixating on problems. Why might someone actively seek out problems, you wonder? In my experience, problems often function as a familiar and comfortable space. We can all relate to experiencing problems and indulging in those negative feelings of self-pity or unfavorable circumstances. However, when we actively seek solutions, it often unravels the underlying causes of those problems, revealing deeper-rooted issues and allowing the problems to dissipate while solutions emerge. Solutions, akin to the comfort zone of problems entail change and the discomfort it brings. While discussions often revolve around comfort zones and familiarity, the conversation rarely touches upon the discomfort and transformations that accompany change. If more people comprehended the positive aspects of change, I believe they would be more open to embracing it.

With the rise of social media and the Internet, it seems evident that there's been a decline in intellectual engagement. Many individuals seem hesitant not only to think critically but also to formulate their independent thoughts, instead opting to follow the crowd, even if the majority is misguided. Being a problem solver involves fearlessly delving into deeper levels of thought and considering all potential avenues or possibilities.

This pertains to individuals in the world who don't merely attempt; they take action. As we previously mentioned trying often represents merely attempting something, a mediocre approach of throwing an idea and hoping it succeeds. Many are content with conformity, choosing to blend in. However, who desires to be the outlier, the person who stands out willing to take risks and challenge the status quo?

Some friends and I conceived an idea for an event at my venue space, not named "sip and paint," but rather "sip and think." It took considerable time to make people embrace the concept, but I found it truly enchanting and intellectually stimulating. It was a moment of realization about the world we inhabit and the prevailing simplicity in people's thinking that led me to understand the potential significance of "sip and think." The essence of this concept involves enjoying an alcoholic beverage while contemplating a professional painting, aiming not to imitate it artistically but to interpret and express the underlying meaning or concept behind the artwork.

Many individuals I've shared this idea with have considered the concept of drinking and thinking to be unconventional, yet I found it intriguing. While people are under the influence, they often reveal their inner thoughts and I thought it might be an amusing exploration into the depths of each person's psyche. Additionally, this event could offer artists valuable insights into various perspectives which I believe they would appreciate. I soon realized that the success of this event wasn't about the idea being flawed, but rather about attracting attendees who embrace a deeper level of thinking. Side bar note, find your tribe!

- Taking on challenges

This is the true essence of success—embracing challenges. You're saying, "I'm on go ready for anything, throw it at me and I will catch it". When you willingly face challenges, you declare your readiness and willingness to confront anything that comes your way. It signifies a commendable and truly attributable characteristic trait.

When you take on challenges is very important to keep in mind, these particular questions:

Does this make sense to me and is it even worth it? The reason to starting here is because challenges is like risk and reward. We all know that risk and reward come with some form of the unknown with the possible twist of I've always wanted this. Most people who take on challenges look at them as fresh starts, the beginning of something great if achieved. That desire for said achievement outweighs whatever risk stands in front of you!

A fresh start reminds me of a sunny morning, with a great cup of coffee or tea and the world's best breakfast there is to offer with a side of freshly squeezed orange juice. Doesn't that sound great? That is exactly what a fresh start and a reason to begin again feels like. It's like with that amazing breakfast I just described knowing that the day ahead might present challenges, yet maintaining an unwavering optimism that everything will eventually align and result in a rewarding experience. Much like discovering a treasure at the end of a rainbow. I realize that not everyone perceives change and new beginnings in the same light but personally, this is my perspective. Hence, I have no qualms about embracing risk when it's logical and purposeful.

To ascertain its feasibility, it's essential to gauge where you presently stand in comparison to your desired destination. Assessing how this newly assumed risk contributes to reaching that goal and whether the end achievement justifies the hardships faced during the process is crucial. It's like analyzing a business's profit and loss statement when contemplating an acquisition; if the profit significantly surpasses the losses, it often leads to considering partnership or purchase. Similarly, in real estate, evaluating a multifamily property involves factors like a favorable home inspection report, an accurate appraisal, tenants with a consistent rent payment history and robust rental incomes that comfortably cover mortgage payments and expenses. Such elements contribute to deeming it a prudent investment. This is precisely what I mean by "making sense" – a comprehensive evaluation of whether the pursuit aligns with your goals and offers substantial benefits relative to the challenges involved.

Entering into new challenges with the perspective that challenges serve to fortify character and resilience is incredibly beneficial. Once acquired, these attributes become enduring qualities that assist in navigating various life situations. This to me is already a win. Having the assurance especially in possessing the resilience to overcome adversities, fosters a genuine belief that numerous things can unfold favorably. Recognizing that nothing is truly a failure indicates a profound comprehension of life's mechanisms. Referring to Ice Spices' lyrics in the Bikini Bottom song "how can I lose when I'm already chose," may seem like simple rap lyrics at a surface level but for contemplative individuals like myself, it resonates deeply. Ice is essentially expressing that if one is destined for greatness and even in adverse circumstances learning and growth persist leading to the realization of one's dreams, then there's no real loss. When contemplated in this manner, it becomes an anthem of resilience and unwavering determination.

If there is any take away from this chapter it would be that the confidence to hold your head high regardless of the success rate is most people's recipe for achieving greatness.

When you look at the lives of many successful figures, it becomes evident that none of them reached greatness without encountering failure, doubt, fear, criticism, opposition or setbacks. Thus if they could confront life's challenges and attain success, the underlying message of my book is that you can do the same. Success leaves clues, you just have to be on the path and be intentional with learning from both the minor and major clues encountered along the way.

Self-Awareness Questions

#INSURETHEDIFFICULTBAG

1. Are you currently harboring what doesn't belong to you emotionally?

____

____

2. Mentally or physically list challenges that are preventing your forward movement.

____

____

3. What are the solutions to your problems?

____

____

4. Would taking on challenges allow further growth in your life or business?

____

____

"Obstacles don't have to stop you. If you run into a wall, don't turn around and give up. Figure out how to climb it, go through it, or work around it."

– Michael Jordan

The Fearless Bag

The answer is either yes or no,
what's the fear in that.

Becoming fearless is a journey that evolves with time and experience. While I've possessed bravery throughout fearlessness wasn't immediate. Achieving fearlessness demanded a deep connection with myself acknowledging my capabilities and disregarding external opinions. What triggers our fears in life? Often, it's the concern about the judgments of loved ones, societal perceptions and the immediate intimidating nature of certain situations. Although this chapter might comprise the concept of fearlessness my focus lies on the primary source of fear which in my opinion, is the apprehension surrounding taking risks.

Though risks and challenges differ significantly, many individuals tend to conflate them. A risk primarily involves the likelihood of a situation resulting in a negative impact, while a challenge pertains to dealing with a difficult situation that might affect your objective. The reason behind their interchangeable perception may stem from viewing a risk as a challenge one willingly embraces, as opposed to an action pursued for an uncertain outcome. Challenges involve engaging in tasks that might not be as straightforward or easy as anticipated but are undertaken with the intent of accomplishment without necessarily considering risk factors.

In the preceding chapter our focus revolved extensively around challenges, understanding their nature and exploring effective strategies to tackle them. In this chapter, my aim is to delve deeper into the realm of risk-taking. To commence, let's explore the distinction between low and high risks. A low-risk scenario typically carries a reduced likelihood of causing significant effects, while a high-risk situation entails the opposite - a higher probability of significant impact.

When contemplating a risk such as embarking on a business venture, I'll use it as a prime example. Suppose you opt to initiate a business. The ideal method to assess this risk involves considering the following questions:

- What type of business should I open?

- How profitable will the business be?

- What would my startup capital look like?

- How much do I currently obtain?

- Do I need and will I be able to obtain loans?

- Can I open, manage and sustain this business as an individual or would it be best to collaborate with a partner?

- Will I need an immediate team or is this something that I can work by myself to have more profits to start?

- Financially what is the longevity of this business?

- Is this a business that is easily able to be sold?

- What are my short term and long-term goals and does starting this business align with them?

Numerous other inquiries can be posed before launching a business and the aforementioned ones serve as an excellent starting point. I chose to highlight these questions initially to foster a clearer comprehension of the distinction between low risk and high risk. This understanding will enable me to offer more descriptive examples pertaining to both categories.

A business could be classified as low risk if I possess existing capital, can efficiently manage the business independently without an initial team or if it doesn't demand a physical presence among other factors. Conversely at a fundamental level, commencing a new business might seem high risk if I lack capital, support or need an extensive team that exceeds my financial capacity and other similar constraints. Embracing risks is inherently beneficial as it contributes to personal and professional growth. Without undertaking appropriate risks advancing to the next level becomes significantly challenging.

Various life situations involve taking risks such as entering into a new relationship. When starting a new relationship, integrating one's life with another's becomes necessary encompassing aspects like finances, mental alignment and more. Factors like differing religious beliefs, family dynamics and career commitments require consideration. In this scenario, risk mitigation takes on a distinct approach by evaluating compatibility between the two individuals' goals and potential challenges that may or may not disrupt current life circumstances. Nonetheless, this risk is imperative for the pursuit of a successful marriage.

Another pertinent example could involve deciding whether it's the appropriate time to buy a home. While considering the idea of purchasing a home, one must also evaluate financial aspects such as affordability of the down payment, potential borrowings from family or friends and the ability to sustain monthly mortgage payments. Venturing into a home purchase without a clear plan for these elements amplifies the risk of losing the property and worsening one's situation. Hence, life isn't solely about taking or avoiding risks but primarily about managing risks effectively and making informed decisions tailored to one's specific circumstances.

It's crucial to acknowledge that not every circumstance necessitates adopting a high-risk or low-risk approach. Each situation varies and the decision to take risks should align with one's individual perspective. Personally my risk mitigation strategy revolves around a three-step process. Firstly, I evaluate if the goal is achievable for me. Secondly, I assess its potential longevity considering whether longevity is a requisite for that particular risk. Lastly in business matters, I contemplate the financial viability of the situation before diving in. By simplifying my decision-making process with these three questions I can efficiently determine whether to engage in or abstain from a situation long before classifying it as low or high risk.

Applying this risk mitigation approach has enabled me to make swift yet astute decisions. I've adopted this method recognizing that not all opportunities allow ample time for contemplation. If faced with a scenario demanding quick thinking, I rely on this process. Even when I have the luxury of time, I integrate this approach while considering whether it falls under low or high risk. Enhancing the skill of risk mitigation stands as a pivotal aspect of achieving success in any endeavor. As previously mentioned, embracing risks is fundamental to success. I encourage everyone to refine their ability to manage risks effectively and swiftly ensuring they capitalize on opportunities without hesitation.

I've been told that I tend to make rapid decisions, which some may perceive as hastily made choices. Yet considering the pace of life and the constant competition surrounding us, time isn't always a luxury one can afford when making decisions. Life progresses swiftly and it doesn't wait for anyone; we share it with others whose lives also move forward. Admittedly, there have been numerous instances where I've overlooked opportunities because I hesitated to decide or quickly realized it wasn't the right fit. However, this often speaks to my proficiency as a decision-maker. I possess a skill for forecasting potential outcomes, projecting the future's probabilities and assessing the paths that lead to those outcomes. This ability to project doesn't entail foreseeing the future; rather it involves foreseeing potential future scenarios based on the present.

If you're familiar with the phrase "the road less traveled," you likely grasp the concept of swimming against the current. Both expressions suggest that while we all have destinies to pursue we don't necessarily need to follow the same path. In my decision-making process, I opt for the less congested route emphasizing the importance of staying in my lane where there's minimal traffic. This advice holds significant weight because a less crowded path usually leads to a quicker arrival at one's destination. Although the road less traveled also presents more challenges and difficulties deterring many from venturing upon it. Embracing this notion early in my entrepreneurial journey acquainted me with gracefully handling challenges, conquering them and effectively managing risks. While most people shy away from challenges due to their inherent difficulty learning to navigate through them with grace positioned me a step ahead in my journey, a principle I acknowledged from the start.

At 23 years old I acquired my insurance license, realizing that despite it not being the most glamorous or entertaining profession for someone my age I devoted myself to understanding the industry's dynamics, both in the present and the future. Observing that the majority of insurance agency owners were typically 50 years old or older, I delved into statistics to discern the typical age range when these professionals entered the field. Discovering that agencies tend to be sold after approximately 30 years and most sellers were in their 60s or 70s I understood that they likely began around the age of 30. Mitigating this risk involved assessing the time required to obtain my license, grasp the industry's intricacies and strategize how to eventually own my agency. It's worth noting that while I commenced my journey at 23 I didn't immediately launch my own agency at that age.

Hence, I needed to calculate the duration required to become proficient in the field by immersing myself as a learner while working as a sales producer in someone else's agency. This experience was crucial in comprehending the operations of running an insurance agency. Assessing the situation, I concluded that this approach carried minimal risk considering my age of 23. I estimated I had around seven years ahead of me before venturing into owning my agency. This timeframe would allow me ample opportunity to prepare, acquire my license, gain field experience and potentially ascend within an agency to gain a deeper understanding. True to my plan, I dedicated approximately two years to tasks like handling calls thoroughly acquainting myself with the products and solely focusing on sales.

I aimed to understand the essential aspects of the back-office operations within an agency; crucial activities such as answering the phones, taking messages and putting client information into the system, learning the system, each individual insurance product and how that pertains to each client's needs and most importantly how to sell insurance effectively and in abundance. I secured a role at another agency, this time as an office manager. In this capacity, I not only learned how to train others in the nuances of the job but also gained firsthand experience in the administrative functions crucial to running the agency effectively becoming the principal aide to the agent.

However, solely possessing those skills wasn't sufficient for me to view the next opportunity as a low-risk venture. During my tenure managing an insurance agency at 25- 27 years old, I was presented with the chance to acquire my own agency that already boasted a staff. While evaluating this risk, I realized that despite the favorable circumstances, I lacked the necessary mental maturity to shoulder the responsibility independently. This particular agency was generating a monthly net income of $10,000 after expenses and employed five proficient and licensed producers. Although to someone else this seemed like the ideal opportunity, I recognized that diving into this venture without the mental fortitude to lead it would likely lead me astray. It might not have yielded the same level of success as initially perceived.

As previously mentioned, I have experienced occasions where opportunities slipped away, yet fortunately even better ones eventually materialized. The next chance to establish an insurance agency arose when I turned 30, this time with a partner. Initially I perceived this opportunity as carrying minimal risk. However, the only downside lay in the fact that I hadn't known my partner for an extended period.

This lack of history with my partner meant uncertainties regarding her work ethic, financial contributions, skill set, plans for agency growth and operational strategies. Despite these uncertainties, I decided to proceed only to realize that the risk was more significant than anticipated.

It necessitated putting my real estate career on hold and navigating challenges related to understanding my partner, managing our differing personalities, work methods and aligning our long-term business objectives. Although the partnership didn't yield the expected outcome, I managed to pivot and shape the agency into its current form. These experiences illustrate the strategies I've shared in this book which I've employed in navigating my professional journey. Now I extend these same tools to you.

Embarking on the insurance agency venture alongside a partner presented financial hurdles. Yet had I shielded away from that risk, I wouldn't have uncovered my potential as an agency owner. The experience of leading a team under my own agency's banner marked a pivotal juncture in my journey laying the groundwork for the next phase of my life. Initially, the insurance domain wasn't a part of my long-term blueprint. However, by embracing necessary risks, navigating through ensuing challenges and adapting continuously I experienced significant professional development. This growth although different from my envisioned path to financial success, aligned seamlessly with my overarching life objectives.

As you manage your business, the ongoing process involves assessing risks and selecting the most favorable course of action. The perpetual pursuit of growth, progress and occasional repositioning is inherent in all businesses. Consequently when faced with fresh opportunities, I apply a set of specific questions to evaluate their compatibility with my current business.

- How does this benefit me or my business?

- What is the level of difficulties involved

- How sustainable is it once achieved

- What does growth look like within it

- Does it align with my overall goals

- If it goes wrong what are the next steps

I consistently adhere to these steps until I attain the ultimate objective for the company. Additionally, there are occasions when my goals undergo significant changes, straying from the initial plan. Yet, I apply these very processes throughout to propel myself to the subsequent level. I don't perceive risk as something to fear, rather I view it as a crucial element to progress to the next phase, particularly when I sense stagnation in the current phase. It's akin to exercising because it's vital to move one's body and sustain a certain level of health. I regard this in the same light as an essential element in shaping my future well-being.

Looking back, what exactly instills fear in us? Whether it's about taking risks or making decisions, whatever unfolds was destined to happen and what doesn't transpire might not have been intended for this moment or perhaps not at all. When you view your life through the lens that what's meant for you won't pass you by and what isn't meant for you will miss you, your perspective shifts significantly. This mindset aids in appreciating where you currently stand rather than constantly fixating on where you aspire to be.

Through life's lessons, I've come to realize that reality doesn't always align with my expectations; sometimes it surpasses them while other times it presents more challenges. Nevertheless, I acknowledge that each encounter positive or negative, guides me along the right path. I rely on my intuition as much as possible and seek guidance from a higher power to navigate my journey. Embracing these elements aids in comprehending and allowing life to transition as fate intends. This realization prevents me from dwelling in the fear of the present or the future as I firmly believe that what's meant to happen will happen. I'm confident that my adaptability will consistently lead me toward a favorable destination in the long run. A track record that has been proven in my life!

Keep in mind that I am not fearless without a plan, I'm fearless because I have a plan; many of them!

Self-Awareness Questions

1. What are you most fearful of and why?

   ____

   ____

2. Name a moment when fear held you back and you later realized it wasn't for the best?

   ____

   ____

3. Try daily small ways to instill fearlessness in your journey. Even if it's a solo date for example, when you're used to being in a group setting.

   ____

   ____

4. Take a moment to view fearlessness as being free. What does that encompass to you?

   ____

   ____

"I have learned over the years that when one's mind is made up, this diminishes fear; knowing what must be done, does away with fear."

Rosa Parks

The Saucy Bag

As you approach the peak of success and sometimes even before, you frequently encounter the question: "who does he or she think they are?" I believe that whenever this question arises in your life it signifies that you've made some significant strides. I've personally been familiar with this question for quite a while likely even before embarking on my entrepreneurial journey; there might have been an aura or presence that I unknowingly projected.

Frequently, this question can be bothersome yet upon reflection within its context, it holds a rewarding aspect. The concept of others viewing you as superior which sparks this question, aids in grasping the notion of "it's not you, it's me"—or in this scenario "it's not me, it's you." Their issue not yours, stems from the fact that you likely never asserted superiority over them; it was always their insecurities surfacing. Regrettably, everyone is accountable for their thoughts and actions regardless of feeling provoked mentally by their chosen perception of others.

The objective of this situation revolves around an individual possessing a specific level of confidence, grace and expertise that others making the statement simply lack the knowledge of how to acquire or embody. It's not a moment for introspection to find faults or "humble oneself," but rather a chance to learn to always maintain belief in your capabilities despite attempts by others to dim your light.

Though it might not be advisable to burden oneself with an excessive ego, there can be a negative connotation in the act of humbling oneself. What humility means is having or displaying a modest or diminished estimation of one's own significance. Similarly, it's often taken as refraining from showing off, prioritizing giving to others over oneself and simply avoiding boasting about achievements, possessions, connections or identity. Yet, I believe humility can encompass understanding that what God grants, He can also take away and that's it. Versus using humility as a tool to uplift others by downplaying yourself.

While it's crucial not to excessively indulge in self-importance it's equally vital not to diminish your worth or identity solely to uplift others. The key lies in not eliminating ego entirely—having a healthy ego is acceptable but rather not allowing it to dominate. Allowing ego to steer can lead to an exaggerated sense of importance, thereby devaluing and disparaging others. Life presents a balancing act of recognizing your own identity and worthwhile also acknowledging the greatness in others.

Since childhood my father bestowed upon me the moniker "the real Mckoy," embedding this mindset within me from an early age. Consequently, my ego began to take shape during my formative years. What exactly constitutes ego? It's a person's perception of their self-esteem or self-importance quite contrary to humility. Therefore, we can comprehend that ego can actually be beneficial. In a world where many individuals grapple with low self-worth, contemplate suicide, battle deep-seated depression and lack the motivation or hope to progress in life, a balance of individuals with strong and healthy egos becomes imperative.

Individuals with robust egos typically assume leadership roles, becoming sources of inspiration and motivation for others. While some may take offense at another person's level of ego, many actually rely on the strength of such egos to propel themselves forward. If you possess a strong ego it's advisable to concentrate on aiding those who require your guidance rather than engaging with those who vie against you or might harbor animosity towards you.

- The Real McKoy in you (by definition)

As previously mentioned, my dad christened me as "the real Mckoy" and he also provided me with a profound understanding of why he used that term. I'll delve deeper into its significance and originality later as my dad isn't the originator of this term. However, his explanation to me implied that being the real Mckoy signified greatness, empowerment to achieve any life goal and an unstoppable determination when driven by a strong desire. As a father, he was merely expressing to his daughter the art of carrying herself with dignity and confidence as she journeys through life and there's nothing wrong in that guidance. In fact, I'd like to believe that while the essence of the Real Mckoy is within me, it's present within everyone regardless of their last name.

While my dad might've been a little on the cocky side, my mom was probably what you would consider a little bit more of a humble person. My mother definitely taught me that I was too good for a lot of things but also that there was a whole world with people in it outside of myself. This taught me the importance of acknowledging others and helping others along the way in life but to her only those that "deserved it," again a balance.

———My mother's teachings emphasized the importance of how you treat others while also highlighting the significance of how others treat you. This reminds me of a video featuring Daymond John from Shark Tank. He shared an incident where he introduced his daughter to a famous rapper backstage requesting a picture or autograph for her. The rapper declined rudely treating them dismissively. Later in his career, Daymond encountered the same rapper as a peer. He reflected on the experience, advising practically to be cautious in how you treat people while advancing as you might encounter them not possibly on your way down but continuously on your way up.

Upon hearing that video, it resonated deeply with me because it presented a different angle on a familiar statement. Typically, the advice goes, "be mindful of how you treat people on your way up as they may be the same people you encounter on your way down." This original notion remains valid as circumstances can reverse unexpectedly. However, the altered perspective—urging caution in treating others on the way up because they may still intersect with your upward trajectory—held a unique significance. To me, it highlighted the importance of treating everyone well irrespective of their status as those at the bottom could surpass expectations and grow beyond what one might anticipate.

That's why it is crucial never to limit someone's potential, nor allow anyone to constrain yours. Our destinies are already written by God, and no human holds more power than Him. When considering how God creates humans, we all start with a blank slate at birth. No one instinctively declares, "that baby won't achieve anything in life" or "that baby lacks what it takes to succeed" or "that baby won't surpass those others." Yet as adults, it's peculiar how we can project such limiting beliefs or ideologies onto each other.

Given life's unpredictable twists and turns, it's challenging to confidently ascertain someone else's potential especially when it's beyond our control. This dilemma often arises from ordinary individuals feeling empowered to dictate another person's fate, resembling what's termed a "God complex." This term draws parallels because as previously mentioned, only God has the authority to direct each person's steps since He is our creator. Personally due to my strong faith and reverence for God, I wouldn't attempt to assume a role rightfully His, as doing so would signify a moment of forsaking Him potentially impeding the blessings He has in store for me.

This all goes back to not internalizing other's opinions on yourself because while people are imperfect, being imperfect they don't always discern what's right or act accordingly. It is not any individuals job to take on the burden and insecurities of other people. This is why maintaining some level of ego is imperative to an individual's well-being.

When we dedicate ourselves to those who seek or desire our assistance it's essential to consider the limit of our help, ensuring it doesn't become detrimental to our own well-being. Have you ever heard the saying, "you can lead a horse to water, but you can't make it drink"? To expand on modified versions of phrases, I'd like to emphasize: "you can lead them to the well, but will they drink?"

Walking someone to a well without being able to compel them to drink implies offering an opportunity without the ability to force someone to embrace it. Contemplating whether they will drink after being led to the well signifies that providing an opportunity doesn't guarantee their acceptance of it. Thus, it's a clear illustration that offering assistance doesn't always result in a joyous outcome.

You shouldn't exhaust your sincere efforts on those who don't appreciate or deserve them. It's crucial to identify individuals seeking genuine assistance, respecting your advice and valuing your time. While helping others it's important not to expect anything in return, but it's natural to anticipate gratitude. Logically why wouldn't one be grateful for any opportunity, particularly when the person giving their primary focus are for their own concerns? If you encounter someone willing to consider you by using their resources, knowledge or simply including you in their life, expressing gratitude would be greatly appreciated.

Understanding that I can't control others has taught me to not get upset with how people react to the opportunities, kindness or grace I offer them. I've come to realize that some individuals aren't ready for change or personal growth at their current phase in life. Therefore, the only aspect I can manage is myself and my actions leading me to accept this reality and withdraw my efforts. Opting to disengage stems from the understanding that providing extensive assistance can become draining when not appreciated or reciprocated. I find solace in acknowledging that only individuals themselves possess the power to alter their circumstances; no one else can aid them without their cooperation. This belief aligns with the notion that "God helps those who help themselves."

- Too much sauce or not enough?

Similar to my own experience when you deeply enjoy being exceptionally helpful, resourceful and deriving genuine joy from assisting others in various ways, it becomes challenging to shift focus from that role and concentrate on self-growth. Embracing personal development and taking pride in your achievements is a significant shift from this stance. Letting go of insecurities and elevating yourself is a natural progression when you choose to redirect efforts away from aspects that no longer benefit you. Making such a decision isn't simple because determining what no longer serves you can be a complex task.

You might believe that a situation benefits you in some way or still serves a purpose but it's crucial to consider what your ideal life entails and whether those individuals or elements align with that vision. Viewing things from this perspective often reveals that many of those components do not contribute to your betterment. This realization leads you to acknowledge that you deserve better than certain things and certain people. It doesn't imply considering yourself superior, rather it signifies that whatever value they bring might not be sufficient to align with your aspirations or preferences.

Navigating through others' insecurities regarding your confidence can significantly dampen your spirits. Particularly when you harness your confidence as a means of resilience and determination. Personally, my confidence stands as my most significant asset. I take immense pride in it because acquiring this confidence was a lengthy journey. While many people express admiration for my confidence, only a few comprehend the effort it took to reach this point.

I haven't always been the most self-assured individual and even now, I still grapple with insecurities. However, I believe that my confidence stems from recognizing and acknowledging my capabilities. These abilities constantly amaze me and keep me challenged, strengthening my belief in them. I strongly adhere to the principle that my competition isn't with others, instead it's an internal contest with myself. I compete with the version of myself from yesterday and certainly with who I used to be years ago because to me, success is measured by growth and that's what I strive for—I've always aimed for success.

I believe that our upbringing and life experiences greatly shape the depth and strength of the confidence we display. Take for instance, my upbringing in a military family—we frequently relocated residing on every coast in the United States. Approximately every three years I had to adapt to new environments, make new friends and navigate unfamiliar territories without the presence of our extended family. Growing up in such an environment compelled me to develop courage and self-belief.

I recall a story my mom shared about our move to Washington state when I was around 10 or 11. On my first day of school there, she remembers me heading to the bus stop fearlessly grabbing my book bag and walking out the door. It always brings a smile to my face when my mom recounts that moment because it mirrors my present-day demeanor. I often wonder if at that moment, my thoughts were along the lines of "I have to go to school, I can't be scared!" If my thought process then resembled my thoughts now, I imagine it was quite similar.

Because of those early experiences, my life took a path where meeting new people wasn't a fear but rather a way of life. I never backed down in the face of fear or adversity. Moreover, I didn't dwell on others' opinions as I often didn't even know those individuals. How one is raised, the lessons and the sum of life experiences collectively shape the person you eventually become. Consequently when people inquire about my confidence levels, I find it difficult to articulate because it isn't merely a conscious desire, rather it's deeply ingrained within me. Confidence has never been a choice for me— I have never had a choice but to have it.

While I've developed a certain level of confidence, I vividly recall moments when it wasn't as pronounced. At the age of 20 I obtained my real estate license—a field where most realtors were typically 35 and above, particularly at that time. This situation posed a challenge; encountering a 20-year-old realtor might not inspire confidence in clients entrusting their significant property transactions to someone relatively young. Despite this awareness, I never allowed it to deter me from believing that I could be someone's chosen realtor. Grabbing my business cards, I went off to Walmart distributing them one by one. During this endeavor I encountered a man who actually gave me an opportunity to present my pitch.

Upon presenting my business card he expressed concerns about my youthful appearance and inquired about my experience in the field. Drawing from the earlier advice in previous chapters about pivoting, I did exactly that. I reassured him by explaining that I was a licensed realtor and had the guidance and expertise of both my mother and grandmother who collectively possessed over 20 years of extensive real estate knowledge. I assured him that if any additional support was needed these seasoned veterans could assist me, essentially providing him with the insight of three realtors in one—an uncommon advantage. He laughed and as a result, I secured the job!

During my initial years in real estate I had the privilege of entering a field abundant with mentors and influential figures. Often, I found myself as the youngest realtor in various settings which provided me with the opportunity to learn from seasoned professionals with over a decade of experience notably including my mother and grandmother. Among these individuals there was one realtor, Valerie Hunter Kelly who particularly inspired me. Valerie a black woman, held the esteemed position of being the top realtor in the state. Notably she led the number one real estate team in the state as well. One valuable piece of advice she shared about dealing with competition especially those selling similar services, resonated deeply with me: "No one else is you, and that is your power!"

She expressed how despite other realtors in the state possessing the same licenses, access to the MLS and resources from similar real estate companies and brokers, she never felt intimidated. Her comfort in her abilities and her self-assuredness were such that she could freely share her strategies without feeling fazed. She firmly believed that she was unique—her essence, her style was her strength and no one could replicate it. Although this remarkable woman has passed away, I'll always cherish the profound impact she had on me as a young adult navigating the real estate industry. Her influence perhaps unknown to her, continued to shape my life long after our encounters.

I live my life with those sentiments that I am, Ashley "the Real Mckoy" and am the creator of all things me as well as, the things that I create and no one else can replicate my essence because after all, who else embodies me but myself? I know for a fact that I will be everything that I am supposed to be and am fully confident in all of my abilities to be. I'm confident in my abilities as a person, a woman, a businessowner, daughter and God willing, future mother and wife to be, etc. And there is nothing and no one that can get in the way of me achieving all that I am here to do in any capacity, I just simply won't let it be.

83

Self-Awareness Questions

1. Do you have too much sauce or not enough?

____

____

2. What are some of your most definitive moments that exuded your confidence?

____

____

3. When you're not confident ask yourself why not be confident instead?

____

____

4. Positive affirmation: I am the Mecca and creator of all things me, who else could fulfill my destiny?

____

____

"Regardless of how you feel inside,
always try to look like a winner. Even
if you are behind, a sustained look of
control and confidence can give you a
mental edge that results in victory."

–Diane Arbus

The Legacy Bag

HIStory became HERstory.

I'd like to begin this chapter by recounting my grandfather's journey in the insurance industry. Without his narrative my own story wouldn't exist. Transitioning from being a shoe shine, he embarked on an insurance career leveraging his knack for exceptional customer service honed while shining shoes for men in elegant suits and impeccable appearances.

Upon venturing into the insurance domain he rapidly ascended to a prominent position becoming a Vice President at Life Equitable, a life insurance company. He oversaw a large workforce and graciously met his wife during this time. By 1986, he opted to establish what is known as a captive insurance agency. For those unfamiliar a captive agency operates under a major brand, while an independent brokerage agency represents multiple companies. The agency he founded in 1986, named "The McKoy Agency," was situated in Manhattan's Upper East Side partnering with Allstate Insurance Company under the heist.

Through this agency he and his wife oversaw the administration of thousands of policies catering to renowned celebrities, athletes, political figures and others. I have vivid memories of my childhood, visiting my grandfather's agency in Manhattan. Upon entering the elevator you'd press the button for the McKoy Agency and when the doors slid open, it was to the office directly. As a young girl, I distinctly felt my grandfather held a presidential stature. His office exuded an ambiance reminiscent of a prestigious and exceedingly pro-fessional institution akin to a Bank of America or any other esteemed establishment.

Along the walls were photographs of the esteemed clients insured through our family's agency. Witnessing this display filled me with immense pride and admiration, particularly observing the genuine relationships my grandfather culti-vated with his clients. He was a remarkably shrewd busi-nessman fostering profound connections with each client, extending even to personal levels. So much so that John Starks from the Knicks became my uncle's godfather due to their bond. To me, my grandfather epitomized success; he navigated business with utmost seriousness and I aspired to emulate his approach and determination!

Through much of my teenage years, I often expressed to my grandfather my desire to join the Agency. However, he consistently emphasized the necessity of attending college making it clear that the insurance agency wouldn't serve as a shortcut for me to circumvent higher education. At that time, his stance greatly frustrated me as I couldn't comprehend why he wouldn't provide me with an opportunity. Presently, I realize the paramount importance of obtaining a college education shaping the experiences crucial for my growth into young adulthood. Furthermore, I came to understand that while insurance might be perceived as a skilled trade, my grandfather held our agency to a distinct and elevated standard not merely as a run-of-the-mill insurance firm.

Following my grandfather's guidance, I pursued a college education as advised. However one day, my grandfather sold his Allstate agency for a substantial sum. This event triggered a range of emotions within me—I grappled with a sense of missed opportunity, feeling that I could have contributed to that remarkable legacy. It also dawned on me that the chance to work alongside my grandfather and absorb the intricacies of the business had slipped away. I used to tease with my friends saying that if I amounted to nothing in life, I could always fall back on working for my grandfather. But in that moment, it felt like that option had been irrevocably taken from me.

During the summer of 2012, my grandfather called me with unexpected news—he was planning to establish another insurance agency, this time in South Orange, New Jersey where he lived. Two years earlier, I had recently acquired my real estate license and had been practicing successfully in Tennessee. He mentioned that the CEO of Farmers Insurance a California-based company, had flown him out to Los Angeles for a crucial meeting. During this meeting, the corporate executives at Farmers Insurance urged my grandfather to emerge from retirement, seeing him as the ideal candidate to spearhead their New Jersey initiative in bringing Farmers to the East Coast. I couldn't help but recognize this as an incredible opportunity for my grandfather, once again reaffirming my pride in his esteemed standing within the insurance industry.

Much to my astonishment, he extended an invitation for me to join him in this venture finally granting me the opportunity to work alongside him. I was exhilarated and swiftly began organizing my relocation back to New Jersey. With my real estate license in hand, I envisioned obtaining an insurance license aiming to become a "double threat." So, I came to New Jersey and became just that! When I started working at the agency, he already had a staff of licensed and experienced agents with an upwards of 10 to 20+ years of insurance experience. This was a little intimidating for me being the sole individual in the office without any prior insurance background.

But in my truest form, I perceived this as a golden opportunity to once again learn from seasoned professionals and embark on my insurance career journey. Initially I held the role of a customer service representative, managing client inquiries and needs that didn't involve policy binding due to my lack of licensure. Despite this, during my regular 9-to-5 hours I dedicated my evenings to studying for my license. I'd diligently study until 2 AM to rise at 7 AM, leaving the house by 8 AM to ensure I reached work by 9 AM. Balancing the demands of learning the trade through practical work experience and absorbing extensive study material was exhausting, yet I was determined to complete this phase knowing it was a crucial step toward advancing to the next role as a Sales Producer.

As I stepped into the role of a Sales Producer, I hit the ground running recognizing that achieving a high level of sales relied on establishing my presence in the insurance domain. Initiating my mission to build recognition, I began by introducing myself and my profession to the individuals at the places I frequented regularly. During my visits to the gas station I wouldn't simply fill up my tank; instead I'd consistently step into the store, whether to purchase a piece of gum or grab a bottle of water making an effort to engage with all the cashiers. My aim was to ensure they recognized me not just as Ashley but also as Ashley the insurance agent, extending these interactions to include the gas attendants as well.

Similarly whenever I visited the local bagel shop for my breakfast sandwich and coffee, I made it a point to inform everyone there about my profession, repeating this routine each time I frequented the place (LOL). At the UPS store I followed the same pattern; at times I deliberately increased my visits purchasing stamps or other items, all to solidify my presence there. Drawing from my experiences in the real estate industry, I understood the paramount importance of consistency and persistently pounding the pavement before receiving a positive response. Eventually, both the bagel shop and the UPS store sought my advice on their policies. I vividly recall rushing back to the office, excitedly informing my grandfather about securing the declarations pages for these businesses. I'd like to think he was immensely proud of my ambition to aim high and that I was getting a handle on things.

I excelled and amassed a considerable customer base during my tenure at my grandfather's agency. I attribute much of my current success as an insurance professional to those foundational years spent working alongside him. Observing my grandfather's exemplary business practices throughout my life shaped my understanding of the high standard required in running my own venture. When I established my agency I realized it transcended personal ambition; I carried the esteemed Mckoy legacy within the insurance industry. These realizations instilled a profound sense of nervousness and anxiety in me as I grappled with the responsibility of filling those significant shoes and the desire to make my grandfather proud.

However, my exposure to the intricacies of entrepreneurship began earlier thanks to my grandmother, who ranked among the top realtors at Liberty Realty in Hoboken during the 1990s. I distinctly recall accompanying my Nana to real estate showings with clients when I was around five years old begrudgingly navigating the staircases of the brownstones—a task I hated. I vividly remember questioning my grandmother about the abundance of stairs as she managed files while various clients joined us. Yet amidst these experiences, my cherished moments involved returning to the cozy office on Washington Street. There, I eagerly awaited the chance to savor the bologna sandwich she always prepared for me patiently waiting as she finished her work.

Those moments held lasting significance and provided invaluable lessons for me. When I eventually became a realtor in New Jersey and embarked on showings with my own clients, a particular day stands out specifically. I recall needing to collect keys from Liberty Realty for my client showings, a moment that illuminated the essence of legacy. Stepping into the office I was struck by the changes; it was a modernized version of the office from the 90s where papers once inundated the desks. While at the front desk requesting the property keys I glanced around, reminiscing about my childhood visits to this very place. Curiously, I inquired about the existence of a basement behind a particular door to which the elderly agent responded "yes, it is actually, how did you know?" Then I proceeded to tell her that my grandmother used to work there in the 90s. This is a true story, the lady covered her mouth in astonishment upon hearing my grandmother's name. She then asked if I was the little girl who used to accompany her. I confirmed that I was indeed the one she remembered, and her reaction was almost emotional as she said, "kids are so impressionable."

Reflecting on the concept of legacy this sentiment precisely emulates the essence of how we perceive it. Legacy is centered around family, children and the inheritance we leave behind for them to cherish once we depart. This is precisely what my family has bestowed upon me, a legacy I deeply appreciate. It's remarkable when someone holds themselves and their impact on you in such high regard, guiding you toward a particular way of life. My family has exerted tremendous effort not only to pave the way for me in various professions but also to set a remarkable example of the kind of person I should aspire to be in all aspects of life.

My family members weren't just professionals or entrepreneurs, they excelled in their respective fields setting the bar at the pinnacle of their careers. Therefore not working wasn't merely a choice, but neither was the option to settle for anything less than greatness. From a very young age the concept of greatness was ingrained in me, even when I lacked a deep understanding of life. It's intriguing to consider that just two years after starting kindergarten, I was already showing homes as a budding future realtor an unforeseen path that no one could have predicted.

I often reference my grandparents because they weren't just an influence on me but also on my parents. Their influence resonated in my parents' careers in real estate, mortgages, insurance and more. We owe this inspiration to the example set by my grandparents, a legacy that transcended two generations. Sometimes we underestimate how observant children are of the adults around them – they keenly observe our speech, demeanor and work habits. As Whitney Houston once aptly said, "I believe that children are our future, teach them well and let them lead the way."

Even though I haven't yet started a family of my own, I envision instilling in my future children the same high standards my family has instilled in me. My parents always emphasized that being the eldest child held significance and that my younger siblings are fortunate to have me as their trailblazer. To me my younger siblings hold a special place in my heart; I consider them my own babies. Their progress and development are incredibly meaningful to me.

I make a conscious effort to recognize and encourage their unique talents while guiding them towards resources that can assist them in pursuing their aspirations. The legacy of my family doesn't conclude with me rather, I am the starting point among the grandchildren. I recognize the weight of this responsibility, considering it one of the most crucial roles I fulfill in life. Being a big sister is without a doubt, my most cherished role.

While exploring the entrepreneurial aspect of legacy, I found myself recognizing the profound impact of my late grandmother Selestine, who passed away in 2021. Her legacy equally influential, significantly shaped who I am today. My grandmother's legacy primarily revolved around family. She was a matriarch to 11 children a family that expanded to include 31 grandchildren, 48 great-grandchildren and 15 great-great-grandchildren. That's a multitude of boisterous cousins, initial childhood playmates, numerous aunts and uncles contributing to your upbringing with a fair share of disagreements, yet an overwhelming abundance of love binding us all together.

My grandmother was raised alongside her sister who incidentally, also had nine children and a multitude of grandchildren. My grandmother expressed that due to not having a large family herself, she aspired to create a close-knit family where everyone would constantly have companionship. That sentiment has stayed with me as she genuinely fulfilled that aspiration. In our family, the reliance on friends was never necessary because there was always a cousin of similar age akin to a brother or sister with whom you could play, form close bonds and journey through life together.

Though I may not personally share the desire for that many children, I am immensely grateful that my grandmother held that vision and successfully achieved her family goals. Her experience has taught me the profound value of having a vast family network, particularly in a world often fraught with chaos. The significance of such a large family lies not only in the occasional disagreements but also in the abundant support it provides. Through my grandmother's teachings, I've learned that love remains the essential element and that kindness, gratitude, grace and being genuine can take you far in life.

Whether those things rooted in entrepreneurial ventures or family-centric principles, I was thoroughly equipped with all the essentials for success in life. I comprehended the significance of family bonds, the essence of love, relationships and friendships and the art of cherishing someone beyond oneself valuing them wholeheartedly. From my experiences I inhibited the lesson of fighting for what you hold dear and continuously striving to nurture relationships, despite disagreements. The wisdom acquired during one's formative years shapes their adulthood and legacy hinges on preserving these learned sentiments passing down these values to future generations, be it your children or those who follow in your footsteps.

In my upbringing, witnessing my grandfather and his wife construct and nurture a prosperous business and family unit together provided a model of a robust and harmonious marriage. Additionally, observing my mother and stepfather adeptly managing a household despite the challenges posed by his military career and deployments to war taught me that a couple can endure and stand united, transcending physical distance and daunting uncertainties. Both these couples instilled in me the aspirations I hold for a future with my husband, aiming to emulate their examples as we embark on building our own legacies together.

Expanding upon the concept of legacy, I want to delve into the significance behind my father's reference to me as the "real Mckoy" and the profound meaning it conveyed about greatness. This term traces its origins to an esteemed engineer, Elijah McCoy. Hailing from Canada Mr. McCoy, a black engineer, relocated to Detroit and invented the lubrication oil essential for today's train and car engine systems. His inventions extended beyond this encompassing creations like the ironing board and lawn sprinkler, amassing a remarkable collection of over 50 patents. Despite his achievements, imitators attempted to replicate his designs. Locals purchasing the oil would specify that it must be acquired from "the real McCoy." This phrase signified that when the product met the McCoy standard, it was synonymous with authentic high-quality excellence.

Understanding my family's lineage stretching back to the 1800s has reinforced my determination to uphold the legacy of McKoy greatness. I feel immensely fortunate to have been nurtured with a strong sense of pride in my family name, instilling within me a profound awareness of who I am as an individual and how I navigate through life. For me and my family the person I evolve into and the impact I create hold significant meaning and significance.

- My big why

In the pursuit of success and greatness, encountering doubts, challenges and various setbacks is almost inevitable. That's why maintaining constant motivation becomes incredibly crucial. In the early stages of my real estate career with Keller Williams Realty, their training consistently stressed the significance of identifying your "big why." Your "big why" encapsulates the core reason driving your actions and defines both the purpose behind what you do and the individuals for whom you do it for.

My primary motivation my "big why," unquestionably revolved around my family. It was the drive to make them proud and extend assistance in various ways – from facilitating job opportunities for my younger cousins to offering references and utilizing my resources. Your "big why" is intended to serve as a continual source of encouragement, pushing you forward during challenging times and serving as a reminder of the initial reasons that propelled you to begin your journey.

While my family comprised a part of my significant motivation, I too, constituted a crucial aspect of my "big why." It's essential never to overlook my nine-year-old self, as that period marked a pivotal moment in my life. It was when I welcomed my first sibling, relocated from New Jersey and had to learn independence at a remarkably young age due to our frequent moves. Reflecting on that young girl who harbored numerous aspirations and dreams about the person she desired to become I recognize that everything I owe, I owe to her.

Over the years I've been fortunate to encounter numerous opportunities, spanning both small and large-scale allowing me to connect with a diverse array of new clients and observers. Establishing this community of supporters has undeniably propelled my business to remarkable heights that I always aspired to achieve. For me these supporters represent another facet of my "big why," as among them are young women who share how I inspire and encourage them to excel in their businesses and lives. Such acknowledgment and gratitude from them are something I deeply treasure and will never overlook. Therefore, I owe it to my supporters to persist in being exceptional, pushing onward and consistently presenting my best self at every opportunity.

For quite some time, I've harbored a strong desire to establish an organization specifically catering to young girls especially those who, like me, may have encountered mental struggles during their upbringing. My own experiences at a tender age dealing with emotional upheaval due to frequent moves, difficulties in forming lasting friendships and the lack of stability by relocating frequently, have underscored my most profound aspiration in life: the need for stability. I am keenly aware that similar to myself, there are other young girls in need of a support system a safe space that resonates with them, fostering a community dedicated to uplifting their dreams, aspirations and true identities. Hence, I embark on this journey not just for myself but also for these young girls, aiming to build a haven that supports their growth. Therefore, I do it for them as well, for the future supporters that I have yet to meet.

Self-Awareness Questions

1. When you go, what do you want your legacy to be?

____

____

2. How much of an impact does your upbringing have on your current life?

____

____

3. Strongly consider your inner child when making decisions in your life.

____

____

4. What does legacy mean to you?

____

____

"We build our legacy piece by piece, and maybe the whole world will remember you or maybe just a couple of people, but you do what you can to make sure you are still around after you are gone."

David Lowery

The Brand New Bag

I'm feeling brand new! I'm experiencing a complete transformation! I'm dismissing negative beliefs about myself embracing my genuine abilities, including those that appear unattainable and actively turning my boldest aspirations into reality. I encourage you to do the same! Reaching a transformative phase in life where you feel you have nothing to lose but everything to gain.

That's why this very last chapter is called the "brand new bag" because in every chapter prior were my experiences that led up to how I'm evolving into the next phase of my life. You know when it's time because you sense this readiness for evolution and transition; it's an inexplicable feeling that what you currently know isn't what you've always perceived, prompting a strong desire to alter your circumstances. Even if your situation feels comfortable and pleasant, that comfort can sometimes hinder progress. We often become complacent failing to extend beyond our limits, preventing us from pursuing new goals and embracing a different way of living.

I tend to make significant changes in 5 to 10-year intervals. Typically I set a 10-year goal, representing my long-term vision alongside five-year goals that function as my short-term objectives. You might wonder why five years is deemed short-term for me; I break down these five years into yearly segments. I assess what needs to be accomplished in each of those years to progress towards the five-year goal, which should mark the halfway point to achieving my 10-year aspiration. I gauge and monitor my goals meticulously to ensure their completion. Although they might not always unfold precisely as planned and detours may arise, breaking down my goals in this manner accommodates setbacks allowing me to realign and ultimately achieve them.

Throughout your 10-year plan it's highly probable that you'll encounter numerous transitions, but for me the most significant shifts consistently occur around the 10-year milestone. Consequently, I begin shedding negative ideologies about myself which involves eliminating pessimistic thoughts or self-criticism and instead, embracing and acknowledging who I am at my current age and stage in life. This practice enables me to perceive life through a fresh lens, adopting a more mature perspective as I continuously evolve with time. It's crucial to occasionally pause, assess how far you've progressed and reconsider your future aspirations because sometimes what we aimed for a decade ago might not align with our ambitions for the next.

Another significant adjustment I often make involves ending toxic and insignificant relationships in my life. While evolving and transforming, certain people, environments or elements that I've been accustomed to might no longer align with the direction I'm moving in. It's not always necessary to discard everything around you but inevitably, there are usually a few elements that need removal to progress further on your journey.

In my experience, it might involve letting go of friendships that no longer benefit me, ending relationships that no longer align with my growth or transitioning away from a job or career that no longer supports my development.

What I've come to understand is that as I continue to grow, learn and evolve in life, I don't need to make as many adjustments to the individuals in my circle or my life. When you know better, you tend to do better and consequently fewer changes are needed in your relationships and surroundings.

Nevertheless, there might be detrimental habits that require elimination for me to progress forward. These could encompass certain traits, actions I regularly participate in or simply lacking the necessary discipline. Recognizing the need to enter the next phase of life and transition can indeed induce fear, but often when you find yourself in that fresh phase, it's truly invigorating.

Eliminating toxicity from our lives is crucial for progress because often, we fail to recognize that our future could stagnate if we don't eliminate specific individuals, things or habits. Embracing change becomes essential when you're prepared to embark on a new phase in life; there are occasions where letting go of everything old is necessary to step into the new.

Embracing and learning lessons from challenging experiences in order to progress effectively was a lesson I had to grasp and accept. It seemed as though I clung to these negative encounters, hindering my ability to move forward due to the fear of potentially encountering similar situations again. Eventually I acknowledged that I might face such experiences again, but this time I would approach them with more expertise or a better understanding having gained valuable experience from the past. Embracing these moments aided in cultivating bravery and a willingness to entertain the idea that perhaps I've genuinely learned my lessons. Now as I advance, there's a better understanding of these experiences leading to a brighter path forward.

Clutching onto past mistakes and misfortunes has never served me well. I understand that unfortunate events can happen to anyone and although life's fairness can be questioned, I've realized that this unfairness shouldn't prevent me from embracing the beauty life has to offer. It has also equipped me with better judgment when encountering new experiences helping me determine if they align with my life, how much importance to assign to them or whether I should engage with them at all, thus potentially risking a recurrence of similar events. Once I attained this level of maturity, I found it pivotal in embracing new beginnings as they arise in my life.

One crucial lesson I've grasped and recognized as an ongoing practice is forgiving myself for enduring certain situations. Understanding that these experiences weren't necessarily life-threatening but rather significant learning curves that persist throughout life. Once I could extend forgiveness to myself for the situations I allowed, it significantly elevated my mental state. This mental shift had the most profound impact on any other state I might find myself in because without a sound mental state, I wouldn't possess the resilience and strength to persistently strive for the life I envisioned.

Once I achieved proficiency in forgiving myself and releasing the weight of negative transgressions, I found myself increasingly enthusiastic about the prospect of letting go and beginning new. The act of letting go and starting fresh transformed from being an inconvenience to an opportunity to make things right this time around. The notion of starting over resonates strongly with the adage "practice makes perfect," emphasizing that often one must repeat experiences before mastering them. This is where embracing the journey becomes crucial.

As you grow accustomed to facing setbacks and persistently attempting to rise again, your comfort and confidence in your capabilities increase. It almost seems like this skill is a prerequisite for mastering such challenges. Without the ability to take risks, endure failures, navigate through unpleasant experiences, interact with unsupportive individuals and potentially fall short of your anticipated achievements, how can one truly comprehend the essence of life's challenges?

The most remarkable sensation during a transition to the next stage is the unfamiliarity of the path ahead where the destination remains a mystery, yet inherently appears superior to the current position. This feeling alone ignites an excitement to my adrenaline fueling my hunger for more and instilling an even deeper, intense passion with each level up. It solidifies my understanding that despite discussing growth extensively in this book, certain aspects of my character will remain unwavering. I'll perpetually uphold my ambition, drive, generosity, intelligence, insatiable thirst for knowledge and aspiration for continuous improvement. These qualities epitomize the tenacity and determination required to achieve genuine greatness.

Initially the concept of "insure the bag" emerged as a playful adaptation of the phrase "secure the bag." To me the distinction was clear: securing the bag meant obtaining it and having it in your possession. While insuring the bag, involved crafting a solid plan ensuring that once you seize and possess it, it remains secured for real. Though I may not be an expert in all areas, my wide-ranging knowledge has been cultivated through diverse experiences at a relatively young age—experiences that go beyond the scope of this book. Despite encountering unimaginable situations, I persevered beyond what many believed possible. Surviving these challenges has proven to me that anything I envision, plan, attempt or dream about is something I can undoubtedly achieve.

This book was not for me to pretend that I'm an expert and know it all and that you should listen to me, but it was put in place for people to know that there is someone who understands just how hard life can be. Someone who has faced moments of profound insecurity, endured ridicule, bullying, oppression, yet remained resilient despite the adversities.

Understanding your identity, principles and aspirations can only be disrupted by your own perceptions. No external force holds the authority to obstruct what God has destined for you; He alone governs your fate. "God is the only one in control of your destiny" is a fundamental assertion that must never fade from your memory. Recall it during challenging times when it seems like the entire world stands against you. Embracing this particular belief is the ultimate assurance in insuring the bag of life!

I encourage you and I urge you to insure the bag when you're on that interview trying to obtain that position.

Insure the bag when you're building up your business and have no supporters and don't know where your next sale is coming from.

Insure the bag when you're hoping for that approval on the home but there's just this one thing on your credit that you have to pay off and don't have the money for.

Insure the bag when your bills are too much to bear.

Insure the bag when all those friends that you thought loved you hated you instead.

Insure the bag when you have that dream relationship going through ups and downs and all it requires is a little effort.

Insure the bag when you want something and you don't want anything or anyone standing in your way to get it.

Insure the bag when you're tired of playing small.

Insure the bag when you got a point to prove.

And...

Insure the bag when you know that you are who you say you are and not who other people want or think you to be!

Self-Awareness Questions

1. Are you keeping track of your life transitions and when they occur?

____

____

2. What does it take for you to bet on yourself continuously and frequently?

____

____

3. Write down a list of old things holding you back from the new.

____

____

4. What does the brand new you look like?

____

____

"Never underestimate the power
you have to take your life in a new
direction."

— Germany Kent

About the Author

Ashley McKoy is a trailblazing entrepreneur whose expertise expands throughout real estate, insurance, and other industries. In the banking, finance, and real estate industries, she is a third-generation insurance agent and realtor. Her tenacity and grit stems from her upbringing with a successful entrepreneurial family whose accomplishments were the gateway for her success. Growing up as a military brat provided her with the characteristic traits of adaptability, awareness, and flexibility in all areas of life.

Being an author has been a long-term dream of hers since the very early age of 9; which is when she started writing short stories, song lyrics, and competing in writing competitions in her local area. Ms. McKoy's enthusiasm for becoming an avid book collector in her youth further expanded her reading and writing comprehension levels; which expanded her vocabulary helping her to express herself so fluently on paper.

At 18, she was offered an internship at a major news and media publishing company; which she declined due to the desire of keepsaking her treasured talent of writing not for profit. However, she often joked that at the end of her working career she would spend the rest of her days writing fiction and nonfiction books at leisure. As it projects, she could be well on her way to achieving that genuine dream. Alongside all of her current career accomplishments, she was selected to be on the Forbes Next 1000 list, and has also had the pleasure of teaching her insurance and real estate skills to an audience of thousands across the country as a public speaker for a few years prior to partaking in completing her debut book.